THE OBAMA CHRONICLES: STORIES FROM THE HEARTLAND:

The Obama Age And Ordinary Americans: A View From The Progressive Side

*This volume is intended to be a snap-shot of the period from
2002 to 2009 inclusive of the rise of Barack Obama, first as a
candidate, and, then his election as President of the United
States. It also examines the Obama style, its origins, textures and
looks at how Obama learned his political style and values in the
context of a specific mix of Chicago values, and those as I
describe as mid-western. The combination of his family's
imparting those mid-western values, and what Obama learned he
needed to do to win in Chicago politics, is and will, be reflected in
how he governs as President of the United States.*

*The book was conceived as an internet-based project, working
collaboratively with over a hundred individuals in interviews, or
who submitted important events in their lives, during this period.
These were transformed into stories by the author. Many were
submitted anonymously and respondents were assured real
names and places would not be revealed. They represent
sentiments, impressions and compilations of many views, but all*

originated with the thoughts of individuals from the period. Most of the final work was done between September of 2008 and March 2009, the intense Obama period.

A third component of the book is my own personnel experiences having grown up in the very neighborhood Obama did his community work. I draw a picture of the Chicago, I believe, shaped Obama's political and social attitudes, and more generally, the mid-western set of values he exhibits. This last factor, I believe, puts into focus the fact that Obama was raised by a heart-land parent and grandparents who imparted mid-western values to the young Obama. These show up in his campaigning and his leadership and decision-making style in my view. I go into detail concerning those values and how they manifested in Obama's approach to politics and decision-making relating them to my own childhood. Obama's Hyde Park is adjacent to my much more modest childhood haunts. I went to Hyde Park high. I walked those same streets he did seeking change. Many in my family still live in the Chicago Obama put his energy into-in his 13 Senate District.
Part compilation, part summary, the book seeks to interweave the reactions of internet participants and what was going on in their personal lives and their reactions to the Obama phenomenon and the rise of the first African-American President of the United States.

I conclude with my analysis of the Obama administration and the challenges the new administration faces. Mid-western heartland politician meets Washington power structure. What happens?

Lonnie Hicks
March 2009

Preface and Acknowledgements

This volume would not have been possible without the heartfelt cooperation of hundreds of individuals who wrote to the author sharing their stories, their best thoughts, their insights and most personal concerns. For the most part it was written between 2004 and February of 2009—the period of Barack Obama's emergence onto the American political scene. Here's to all of those who contributed to this book. I hope I have been true to your sentiments, thoughts, feelings, ideas and contributions.

A special acknowledgment to my family and friends who listened for many many hours to my writing attempts to encapsulate what was being said by respondents and of course these individual themselves.

In writing the book, themes and concerns emerged, many centering on the election, but respondents also discussed their personal lives, their views on many topics ranging from marriage, birth, death, dating, sex and politics. I heard from writers, poets, young people, the elders and individuals from all walks of life and backgrounds.

This book is a compilation of the items I received. I have blended sometimes several points of view into one story to condense items. I have chosen ones which seemed representative or, especially powerful and took from my notes and interviews, emerging themes and transformed what I conceived to their essences, onto a literary platform, artistic license if you will. How well I have done that is for the reader to judge.

In short, this book is not just about Obama, but about Americans as well, their lives, their views at a historic time-the first African American on a path which resulted in his election as President of the United States.

Therefore, this blend of everyday life with the historic time seeks to connect the personal with the historic and hopefully creates a snap-shot of the average American coping with life as Obama emerged. Importantly, this was and is an Obama strategy—has Americans become personally involved in his campaign, his biography and in his Presidency. He sought not only to win an election but, to as well, mobilize a generation.

This is not intended to be a scientific survey; rather it is a literary interpretation at a specific time-period.

My views and my interpretation of the views of others are my own. For the most part I separate the two making it clear when I am speaking my own view.

What is striking to me finally, in looking at it, as a whole, is these statements contain a power, an authenticity, rare in story-telling writings since they originate from real people speaking their mind on issues of paramount concern to them. And hopefully, my insights into the Chicago where Obama learned his politics will add additional dimension to the book.

Growing Up Chicago Style:

My views have been shaped by growing up in the very neighborhood where Barack Obama did his community work and in the state senate district he represented. My dad, 87, still lives in the district on the South side near old Comisky Park, and, carries as knife as a hedge "against the gang-bangers;" did one-handed push-ups until he was 76—"to be in shape if gang-bangers jump."

He calls every woman "baby fox" and every woman loves him for it. He kisses hands, smiles, draws, paints and complains about the "Daly" machine. An activist union organizer, he rose to be the first African-American union vice-president in the steel mills near Gary, Indiana. He is a natural organizer.

He won't leave Chicago to "sit in a big, empty house all day in California," with me and my family. He told me that he is thinking about getting married to his eighty-year old girl friend because "I may be old, but, I am not dead"

He is a Chicago man through and through.

He sits and talks about his Chicago and the Chicago of my youth.

That youth was tumultuous, at once family centered, but, often violent. Gangs, death and fear were common, and, many longed to get out of post World-War II Chicago poverty and the ghetto, and move up.

This Chicago was created by African-Americans who left the South, from Mississippi, New Orleans, or from other Northern cities like Harlem, Detroit or Milwaukee, looking to get good jobs in the slaughter houses of the "city with big shoulders." They came for good railroad porter jobs, and the opportunity to plant their feet firmly on the path to the middle class. My grandfather, on my mothers side, came to pursue his dream of having his own church and he did get his own church, bringing Baptists together on the South side longing to continue that Baptist faith learned in their cities and rural areas of origin.

Every Sunday, my grandmother, his wife, would bring the entire family together for "supper" at 11am. They would linger all day, eating talking, complaining, making plans, catching up and speaking of the black and white worlds they knew.

Black and white because mine is a multi-racial family, whites on my grandmothers side, and, black on my fathers side. The weekly suppers were continual classes in race relations, politics and economics, with both sides making points; talking loud and condemning the Daly machine, white relatives criticizing black America, black relatives criticizing white America. There were complaints about black merchants who cheated their black customers; where food was purchased on credit--at an interest rate--where everyone played the "numbers" hoping to get rich; complaints about the Man, about cheating husbands and straying wives, no good children and the police, always the police.

The neighborhoods were really small towns of five or six blocks. There were Sunday soft ball games in Washington Park each Saturday. Women hid the beer and talked and men pot-bellied to the plate to face Sachel Paige wanna-be's who just happened to be doing soft ball.

There was violence, often neighborhood against neighborhood. I remember a summer night when the call when out that there was to be a fight. Kids were given rocks, shoes and heavy scarp iron and told to go to the roof tops of the three-story walk ups because there was to be a fight.

That night, flickering torches moved down the alley behind our 50th street walkup and 50 to 75 men and boys had come again to destroy a tree-house the group had destroyed the week before. This time there would be a rumble.

At signal I threw a brick. Another one and then another. Screams; yelling; fighting below. Above, we were the artillery, now the ground troops had moved in.

The police, always the police—cruised, looking, demanding that this corner or that corner be cleared. The worse was Two-Gun Pete; two pearl-handled revolvers and over 13 teens shot. He would give only one warning "clear this corner or by the time I come back there will be trouble" And there was trouble, two gun would come back, and, from the car, shoot. Killed thirteen.
Worse, because Two-Gun was black.

The neighborhood organized. Pete came cruising, peering out--issuing his usual warning--but then, there was a woman screaming down a dark alley. "Help, Help, he is choking me." Pete walked into that darkness and windows opened and gasoline poured down-down on Pete; he was wet with it and when he realized the trap he ran for his squad car to make his escape. He was too late. He was lit. He flamed, He screamed.

Miraculously, Pete lived, and came back six months later, with his same swagger. He was trapped in the vestibule of a small apartment building and re-lit. That time he died.

Death was near, always near. I was walking with my friend Larry on a warm summer night, Chicago's famous humidity flaring in August; two men walked toward us--one hit Larry in the chest. Both kept walking as if nothing happened. Larry ran. I followed him puzzled as to what happened. In front of the apartment building Larry was down, bleeding, an ice pick to the heart.

Crazy Horse and the Warriors, a local gang, caught me one night after a basket ball game. They surrounded me. The guy in front had a 2 foot plank with a nail in it. The idea was to bring the plank down suddenly into the top of the skull of the victim. I knew the routine. I looked scared. I was scared. But I remembered my Dad's advice. I kicked the plank-wielder in the shin, grabbed him as he limped and drew him down into a clump of bushes. In the dark of night the gang could not see and I slipped through the bushes bruised and bleeding from tiny cuts, while the guy was yelling to the rest of the gang members to lay off with the kicking.

There was irony too. I had a paper route, my first. I carried over 150 papers which was a huge responsibility for a youth my age. One winter, crunchy snow on the ground, I was finishing my route having collected over 200 dollars. My route ended literally across the street from Hyde Park, the same Hyde Park where the Obama family currently lives.

Hyde Park is the neighborhood of the University of Chicago, of the upper and middle class. There people had money, had large homes, dressed well; mostly white; students. I saw them walking along with books unafraid, not wary, relaxed. It was clear they were not from my neighborhood. There across the street from where my route ended was the world of the middle class world. Across the street was another world.

On my side of the street were three story apartment buildings and poverty. The street was a line. Chicago is full of these lines. One side you see poverty, the other side of the street, the Mayor lives. That Chicago has not changed. This is still my Dad's Chicago. He can see the Mayor's neighborhood from his back window across the alley, across the divide between the Chicago middle class and the poor. That divide is, and was absolute.

This Chicago, in the fifties was the Chicago of Catholic immigrants, many from Eastern Europe. My next door neighbor was Polish, raised corn in his backyard, raised chickens and sold them. It was the Chicago of Poles, Estonians, Latvians, Italians, and Irish--all in that racial melting pot. All ruled over by the Daly machine which, in the absence of social services, provided social services for the new immigrants and the poor. A chicken indeed was in every pot--for your vote. Jobs in the Daly machine were there for you; help with your kid's tuition, for your vote.

In the neighborhoods in those days, there was the rag man to buy your rags, the knife-sharpener to sharpen your knives. And, there was the ice man to fill your ice box each week (no refrigerators.)

The ice man. The ice man. Summer days were hot and the horse drawn ice-wagon would come to deliver ice. Kids, like me, would wait for the ice man to make a delivery, leaving the ice in the wagon unguarded. Ice pick in hand we would climb onto the wagon and chip off the ice and throw pieces to friends below.

The ice man, cameth back, and caught me. I bolted the wagon, ran a safe distance, laughing, stuck out my tongue taunting him. Suddenly, my mouth ran red with blood; the ice man had actually thrown his ice pick and it had gone right through my out-stretched tongue. True story. I still have the hole in my tongue.

My grandmother was outraged. The neighborhood organized and the ice wagon stopped coming to our street. The ice company said it was too dangerous; might lose a valuable horse—because the ice horses were often unhitched, stolen, and taken for a joy-rides.

Neighborhood was neighborhood, turf was turf. You defended your neighborhood.

 In all, this, our multicultural family found time for love, for humor and built family stability in the midst of chaos. Education mattered and was encouraged. Grades at grandmothers were openly discussed and celebrated. Each child got the attention of the adults and praise at Grandma's dinners if the grades were good. Achievements were rewarded with fifty cent pieces and you were told, "now don't spend it, save it, buy a house or get your own business started." I went to Hyde Park High at that time a magnet school for Chicago's best students. That was wildly celebrated in the family. But I dropped out junior year out to go to work for the family-ultimately graduating from night school.

I learned my politics, too, in this environment, my sense of neighborhood, and, my sense of humor.

Chicago-style humor is raucous, direct, scathing and often race is at the fore-front.

I came home from school one day and casually mentioned that one of the school kids had called me a nigger. Dad was pretend- outraged--(I learned later.) He began to question me saying he was going to school with me then next day to question my teachers.

"Who called you that racist name? he began, was it the Chink, The Polock, The Bo-hunk, the Dego, the Spick? I told him to forget about it I did not want him to go to school. He would be an embarrassment. Even at my age I knew you don't fight racism while exhibiting that same racism yourself. But, Dad was having a little fun at my expense.

Humor, I was talking about humor. Lots of humor. You couldn't hear at grandmother's house, sometimes, because the laughter was so loud.

Here is some of the wit and wisdom of my many uncles in pithy over-heard short statements which were so much of my child hood education. Some of it I understood, much I did not. But, you might.

Here is the wit and wisdom of the Uncles:

Don't think too much;
you are not that smart anyway;
day-dream more
that makes you smarter, if you believe in it.
Einstein did. Worked for him.

Don't be too humble
it implies you think you're so great
you need to be.

Don't be too wise;
it makes people nervous;
hold back a little, act like you can learn from other people,
you seem smarter that way.

Don't try to look too good--
people will see you only
as good for looking good.

If you are busy trying to prove
that you are right--
you are probably wrong.

Make one or two good
friends;
too many and you
will acquire enemies posing
as friends.

Tell the truth
and then run like hell
and don't look back.

Don't think too much
about the Future

you'll stumble over Right Now
won't get any Future at all.

Life is like taking a leak;
aim straight
and keep your mind
on what you are doing
otherwise, you pee yourself.

Love your parents
even if they don't deserve it
because you have to have
some love
to give some love.

Remember the golden rule
but, payback is sometimes better.

Don't get all hung up
on bad and good
pretty soon you won't
have any friends.

Kiss and hug
all the children all the time.

People are not a movie.
People are real
and they are not in your movie.

Don't watch television--
cuss television.

You can't be cute
past sixteen.

Don't kiss in the dark
if you are not willing
to kiss in the light.

Wonder why and why
all the time.

 Get an education--
your body wears out.

If you hear gunfire,
ask what it is
five blocks away.

Smile at someone
for no reason
remember how
much it means
when it happens to you.

Don't try to be sexy;
be sexy.

Get low with animals
and children;
get on the floor.

Let someone else
shine sometimes.

Shut up.
You don't have to talk
just because you can.

Don't eat anything
bigger than your head.

Don't eat without chewing your food good.

Control what goes into your body
you are going to need it a long time.

You can beat a gang in a fight
kick the first one in the shin
use him as a shield
big guys can't fight if they's
limping around.

There are only two things
a woman believes that man
says:
You are the most beautiful woman
I have ever seen,
and here's the money.

Nobody is better than you
even if you think so,
and you are no better than
anyone else--
even if you think so.

Want what you need,
and need
what you want
the exception is
the neighbor's wife.

Kiss slow,
run fast,
and play for keeps.

If someone
makes you laugh til you pee
marry 'um.

The difference between
Capitalism and Communism
is that Communism is the
exploitation of man by man.
With Capitalism it is just the
other way around.

You can't go home
if you never come back.

You can get along with people
if you can be alone with people
and keep your mouth shut.

Your life is going to be
engraved on the inside lid
of your casket.
Make it interesting reading.

You can get over yourself
if you face the full-length mirror
turn around
bend over
and look through your legs;

If Jesus came back
he'd go to some churches
and take his money back
and the collection plate too.

If someone calls you a name
ask for details;
"What kind of fat cow?
Do you mean the Jersey?
Holstein?
Oh, you don't know?
then, you are not only mean
but, dumb too
and from what I can see
you ugly too."

You are old if you
don't want to get out of bed
in the morning--and depressed too

The perfect woman wears
a gingham dress;
the perfect man
wears only a smile.

Babies come naked
kids like to be naked.
Grown ups have their most fun naked;
In the grave you will soon get naked.
There is something going on with naked.

When you come home
give a hug and a smile;
don't be a coward.

Kissing a pig
don't make bacon
and kissing rear-ends
don't make friends.

Catch up;
I am so far behind you
I am ahead.

Wearing a watch
don't mean
you know what time it is.

If being rich made you happy,
happy people would be rich
but they ain't
but, they do know something
you don't—misery and rich
is better that misery and poor.

I had an uncle Dan
who always said that a man
had to be taught
how to please a lady

by learning to say 'yes dear'
just like he means it.

I had an Auntie Sal
who always said that a woman
had to be taught how to please
a man
by learning to say 'yes dear'
just like he means it.

If you get down low and depressed
keep digging
because the earth is round
you'll come out the other side
ok.

Remember:
nothing happens
in life
until somebody
falls in love
with something,
or somebody.

Joy is a happy smile
Best be yours.

So in this multi-cultural, multi-racial family humor, plus grandmother's suppers kept us together. And, why grandmother stories here? My mother died when I was nine. I spent years at grandmothers. Even before she died (TB) we kids spent time at her house every weekend. After my mother's death I lived with Lula, (her name,) and gained a sense of her history, of the family history. Of how whites in the family, passers, blacks, American Indians (my great grandmother) lived their lives and coped with a changing 1950's America. I met my great-grand mother. She was 102-- smoked little cigars, had an ear horn and shot imaginary arrows at us kids if we did wrong.

So the family is mixed.
Obama, too, grew up multi-racial family-so did I. Obama was raised by his grandparents. So was I. Obama too, knew the difficulties of having one foot in the black world and one in the white world. So do I. He came to Chicago, to my neighborhood, and, came to understand that world which was my world.

But, here there are more than Chicago values at play. Chicago is part of the mid-west. Mid-western values permeate the Chicago landscape.

Obama came to understand that mid-westerners have values that are different than the Coasts. We have regions in this country and those regions genuinely have different values which are reflected in daily life.

National media homogenizes everything. Most of us have accents and don't talk media-speak. Most of us have different experiences, and, with the advent of fragmented media markets, our differences have become more exacerbated where once media brought us together, allowed us common experiences, where we all watched the same three networks, now that has all changed. I don't have to, if I don't want to, experience anything different than my self and my own views-- and those of others who agree with me. I can talk to; see on television, only those shows and personalities which reinforce my own pre-held values. No melting pot here. Provincialism permeates the right and the left; therefore, the social and political fights become more ideologic, more entrenched. That is not good for America. It is bad for America.

Note that was not 1950's America. Ethic groups lived close; no suburbs yet. We were all together. While the pot was boiling over with tensions these communities knew one another, each culture, each tradition because we all lived in the same poor three story walkups.

So how does Obama fit into all of this? He represents a counter-trend to much of the fragmented, homogenization trend. He represents a counter trend, a thought pattern that seeks to be post-racial, post Democrat-Republican, beyond partisan politics; a common sense, practical politics—one able and willing to take ideas from any one.

Is this true? Is Obama post all this? Unknown at this point. But, then the point is he is expected to be. His back-ground is such that he is motivated to try to bring the races together— blacks and whites. Most multi-racial individuals have this same motivation. I do. He absorbed the Chicago over-lay of those mid-western values he already possessed; and the Chicago style of politics.

Time will tell time if he can accomplish his goals as President; too soon to tell how the Obama story will ultimately turn out.

But, we do know how it began, and this where this book begins; what impact did Obama have, and continues to have, on America coming out of the Chicago caldron, coming from a heavily mid-western value set.

 Lets examine those values in more detail and their role in Obama's style and decision-making process.

Midwestern Values and the Election of Barack Obama:

Chicago, however much seen as a large urban city, nonetheless, sits in the heartland. I remember hog belly futures reports on the radio every day; commodity futures were what the city lived on—plus packing plants and the railroads.

Those mid-western heart-land values are ultimately what catapulted Obama into the Presidency. I share those values. They never leave you.

Obama mother's imparted those values to him as well. Transplanted to Hawaii, his grandparents accentuated those same values begun by his mother. It is no accident he landed in Chicago. Those same values thrive there too.

So it makes sense to ask what are those vaunted mid-western values were as I learned them, and what role did mid-western values play in his election.

The list of values is a long one. Let's get started.

A Love of the Land:

The American Dream is a dream about owning your own plot of land. From the pioneer beginnings to the urban homestead of a white picket fence it has always been about the land. No more so that in the mid-west.

My family had stories about how great-grandfather relatives homesteaded some plot of land, cleared it, identified a source of water, built the barn, built the house, raised the crops or the stock and made his way into the American version of the good life.

Land was wealth, food, energy, family, history, war and peace. In my great grandfathers America the three legs of American prosperity were firmly in place: Cheap abundant, fertile land, cheap labor, and finally, cheap energy.

He and his kin made the prairies fertile, fertile enough still to feed the world; he and his kin provided the cheap labor (slaves in the South) to clear that land and make it fertile, he and his kin utilized cheap energy, steam, oil and coal to fire the furnaces of industry.

But, years later, my grandfather was bitter about it all in Chicago-land. He had seen the family farm taken away from his father and him by high taxes, by land speculators, by the railroads, by the robber barons that took the land away once it was productive, herded him and others like him, to the cities to make a living in the new factories, to pursue watered-down dreams. His was that of founding a church. He and others like him, however, never forgot that their American dream had been supplanted by a factory job, wage-slave living, and Jobism.

This city life was a dependent life, a major disenfranchisement; an abandonment--a broken promise. They talked about all the time at grandma's house. Bit by bit as the great-grandparents died off, I would hear of how the 20 acres were sold off bit by bit to pay off the taxes. How the old farm was dismantled and divided among the feuding children, most of whom wanted the cash--selling out to the banks, or to the developers or to agri-business.. This is still going on in America. The family farm has been factory-ized, big Agriculture rolled over the family farm.

A friend of mine says that the last Christmas in America was 1968, the last time real wages increased in the United States. My grandfather says it was before that when big agriculture acreage was larger that family- owned and farm-farmed acreage.

Midwesterners are serious about the land.

Self-Reliance:

You are taught self-reliance. in the heart-land. As one of my uncles's used to say "only you can get you out of bed each morning"

Family, kin and neighbors can help, but, in the end, it's you, only you, that you can rely on. And, you know, "most times that will be enough, enough to attract the help you need."

Ultimately, that is the Barack Obama message. The election, he is fond of saying, is about the American people not him. He lowers expectations telling the American people they have what is needed to succeed in crisis times.—they have themselves. We are the ones we have been waiting for.

This is not only the message of the organizer, but, a statement that you have to rely upon self to get started, to get organized and march on city hall, to get the changes needed.

As a youth, if I didn't have money to get to school, I walked. If I didn't have money for classes I audited classes and took them later or not at all. You were expected to "make do" and not shrink from defeat or disappointment.

If I lost in love it didn't matter because love was not out there, it was inside. I was always happy inside; therefore, I could never "lose out" on love.

I once romanced a college girl, guitar, bedroom window, rose in teeth--the whole thing--knowing she didn't care a lick for me. And she told me that. I told her that I understood, that I was practicing, getting ready for the girl that did like me. I started to be very attractive to her then. But, it was too late. I got good on that guitar and moved on.

So out of self-reliance and, losing a fear of losing, comes learning. You use failure to learn and you never really lose at anything. From this, the next step is commitment, stick-to-it-ness and a "you don't quit" attitude-coupled with a "you get up and try again" determination. This is rock hard determination is born of pioneer stock and poor people's ability to endure. You endured, because you had to; you dealt with whatever life was dealing.

All of this is accompanied by certain calmness, since losing the prospect of losing is not nervous-making or, is not any measure of one's self worth, there is born a certain confidence. Besides, any member of the family who panicked in a crisis weakened the entire family.

A college room mate of mine was from Nigeria. Mowebe and I roomed at the height of the civil rights movement and I would tease him about his wearing the Nigeria traditional garb, a toga-like affair. I told him I had mixed feelings about it since the Klu-Klux-Klan wore white sheets too.

He said "Lonnie, it's like this. People may call me a nigger, but, since I am not from your country it has no impact on me. You can tell me it is a sheet but, I don't feel it." His point: you can be denigrated, but, whether it works depends upon how much you buy into the insult. You have to believe it a little bit to be insulted. You have to believe just a little bit you are a loser to be affected if someone calls you a loser. You can fight back; it is just harder if you are battling with your own self-esteem at the same time.

So here we are with Obama running a Presidential Campaign which has all the above elements. Organizers were taught to see themselves in charge locally, to take charge, not to wait for headquarters direction. (Contrast this with the Clinton campaign.) Small groups, enclaves and caucus structures in many states perfectly fit this idea and the values which under lay it .Think of Iowa. Obama was a mid-westerner first, and black second, (no matter how others saw him, he did not see himself as a black man running. He was a mid-westerner running; more over, ran a campaign consistent with those mid western values. No accident he won Iowa. It was, and is the values he projects which are the keys. There are others as well.

Resourcefulness:

"No" is only a pause on the way to yes. A sense of empowerment, leads to a confidence that with others similarly empowered, problems will be solved. Resourcefulness is the belief that barn will get raised--if we work at it and count on our neighbors who will come, and, if they don't we will think of something else. This is powerful, "we will think of something." That is confidence borne of small successes, and, an environment where others can act and do act. Obama picked up Roosevelt's New Deal strategies. We try this and if it fails we try something else until we find what works. This is an action orientation, which says, let's not debate what time it is, you don't know and I don't know either. Let's go and have a look at the clock.

This point is important. Much of middle class life to a kid coming from the ghetto is about words, debate, blame and subtle put-downs. In Chicago, you didn't debate, you acted. If a gang catches you on the street, you don't try to reason them out of whipping on you, you act. You have no illusions about the power of your logic to change the street world.

This action orientation is also a pioneer heritage. John Wayne, Clint Eastwood, all action heroes, not talk heroes. Yet, as we can see, action all the time without thinking can be dangerous. Note Obama has learned that lesson from his earlier campaigns where he jumped in races before he was ready and lost badly. Now he is more cautious. But, he has mounted the most ambitious action-plan for America in a generation. Every thing is to be done, not debated.

Family:

The mid-west is farm country, not like the far west mountain country or Hollywood country. Family matters. Often large, (I had seven in my family) each person is very important on a farm. Many chores to do. Kids were needed, loved and an asset, and, absolutely essential to the success of that small farm business.

Contrast this to the modern urban city scene where kids are not essential to the economy of that city. They are ornaments, they dance and sing, look cute for their supper, are crammed up in high schools, kept off the job market and away from competing with their fathers and mothers for jobs. Many are sidelined for much of their productive lives. Even with a college education, they are crammed in a "job-ism" culture with; not only meaningless work--if you can find it--but, work which could easily be done is less expense ways. Urban young people sense they are superfluous--even if working, and, therefore, spend a lot of time on narcissistic pursuits. They can't marry—many don't have the resources to do so-- and, in America, languish away a good deal of their young adult hoods in consumption, reality show hostilities, and confusion. Obama would put them into national service. That is something concrete; skills and self-worth can potentially be gained or regained. The green economy might provide future jobs, but, the boomers still block employment paths to that— especially if they go for green job re-training in their later years. Where are the future jobs for our young?

Young urban people, therefore, have fragmented experiences of life, of how the world works, On a farm kids see birth, death, life, live and work along side their parents. They know the work-world of the farm from an early age and they are essential.

Now, of course, much of that has changed. City kids don't even know what their parents do for a living. They are isolated from the world of work.

Young people in the small farm towns are on the brink of disaster; corn crops have been diverted to ethanol to survive, and there is no real family farm to inherit. Developed out of existence, the young have to leave, take a job at the local prisons or go off to war. And, the towns continue to rust, jobs flee and the hollow faces grow more numerous. Where is the future of the small town?

So family, like the culture, has become fragmented. The kids can't make a living on the farm, flee to the city to find jobs, dooming the tax base and the situation exacerbates.
The poor show up in the cities too--farm girl meet city pimp. Farm boy meet hip-hop and the racism of class clashes grows. Yet, the example of how, even in the urban setting, family can be stabilizing for the poor and the displaced exists before our very eyes. Asians, Mexican-Americans and others with strong family ties band together five to a house, to a room and all work and save and survive. But, before we ask why blacks don't do this too, we have to establish that this family enabled story has flaws too and is not true per se. But, that is the subject of another book.

Now, we finish this topic on family--identifying it as a as a bed-rock concept—one Obama shares, as do many Americans. We see Obama put this image of a stable family at the center of his campaign. Of course, most politicians do. They know Americans long for a stable family even as it is being torn apart by forces they cannot forestall.

Whether his policies will rectify the family situation in America is, of course, another issue.

The Role of Women in the Family:

The role of women in the black family and mine is an example.
A strong grandmother figure gathered the family together,
kept the family together, issued discipline and rewards. Truly a
bulwark.

Struggling against the odds women played and continues to
play a critical role in keeping the black family together.
I remember the talk my father had with me about women. He
called me before a scheduled trip home from college to say he
wanted to have a talk with me that his dad had with him. The
topic was women.

Well, I was fascinated by his suggestion. Dad, of course, I knew
loved women and women loved him. Even though already a
college sophomore, I was interested.
Home, I sat with him and he took a deep breath and began.
'Now keep in mind 'he said. 'women are not like men they are
always thinking, always feeling and they pay attention to
everything. Nothing is neutral when it comes to your female
species.

Now you and us menses can live in caves eating pizza and
would gladly be doing that if we had the chance; women
civilized us introduced us to china, forks and spoons and clean
underwear.

Now your dirty socks you used to piled up in your room, as a
teen-ager, and never wash them won't do if you want to get
married.

Turn your head to special days, birthdays and anniversaries and the day you and your future wife first meet. Your first date. Write those dates down on your forehead. Learn to like all women, but love only The One. Don't even, when dating, sneak a peak at passing Ones.
Don't look too low at the Twins; Don't look too high; rather take it slow and look deep into her eyes. There is where all answers lie. Memorize her face, her lips, times she laughs, times she cries.

Above all understand you have the privilege of living with someone who represents the Superior Ones. Yes, they are smarter quicker, more verbaler and, you my son, are just along for the ride.
They are stronger too. They can work all day at some job on their feet and come home and work all night, while you are flat bushed on the couch with a beer.
Women's are half the planet; cause half the fights among the men because men know they'd be lost without 'em."

Therefore, many black males come from female-headed households and, and largely that remains true today. In the black family, women hold it all together.
In hospital rooms, when death is near, you hear men call from mom, not dad.

Calmness in the Face of a Crisis and Leading by
Example:

The pioneer history of the mid-west remains, in families, in the culture, in daily life, passed down from grand and great grandparents. These farmers and settlers left the east coast, or even Europe, and came here for land. They opened the west, cleared the land, raised the stock and fed the nation. Chicago was the first city many of them knew as they sought to sell their crops and stock, especially after the civil war.

The rigors of frontier living demands, and selects for, certain traits. One's ability to stay calm in a crisis is essential. "No drama Obama" is not an accidental personality trait. Compare this with the shoot-from-the-hip media frenzy and the Washington, react-every- minute-of-every-day-to-everything mentality. Obama has a different style and it is a mid-western style.

The ability to remain calm in a crisis, endure long-lonely hours on small, isolated farms and a strong body able to endure the rigors of the prairie were important. Devotion, steadiness and clear-eyed practicality were traits to be contrasted with city folks who were often portrayed as fops and dandified; women who were mostly interested in prettying up their faces and never knew a hard-days work in their lives.

These are traits Obama projected, steadiness, family-orientation, calmness, and all mid-western. Not exclusively, of course, but, much admired there.

Oratory and More Oratory and The Black Church:

The black community in Chicago, and probably nation-wide, encourages oratorical skills. Rooted in the black church, the preacher's effectiveness is often dependent upon his/her ability to stir the congregation. My grandfather could preach and have members of the congregation speak in tongues, could have individuals get the holy spirit and come to Jesus at the altar. New members were recruited after one visit stirred by the music and the oratory; frightened by the evocations of hell, uplifted by the evocations of the pleasures of heaven, consoled against the here and now--which was often bleak.

The congregation of the poor have their reward in that Jesus understands them, that they, the last, will, one day be the first; that they are the good people, the sacrificing people, the long-suffering, the morally superior, the trampled down, but not beat down. Their turn will come in heaven. The injustices of life will sometimes bring an earthly leader who will set things right. Sometimes, the young however, are impatient don't want to wait on heaven for their reward; they want a leader-hero who can deliver now, right now. That is sometimes a preacher, sometimes a politician, anyone who can paint a picture that it could happen.

I preached in my grandfather's church on occasion, and learned to move a crowd, make of them believers in a high justice, make them believe in themselves and their own abilities to free themselves from the restraints of poverty, of the oppressive atmosphere of the police. This later training ground became part of performing poetry with the same kind of energy, fervor and communicativeness.

Obama spent 20 years in church learning and observing what works to move people to action. Churches are community organizations and community organizers. They hired Obama to do community organizing. This is the black politician's natural classroom, the black church.

But, oratory is more than power-speak in Chicago, and, in black communities, across the nation, language skills are what poor people learn because, often, all they have is their bodies and their voices. Learning how to be a powerful speaker had several origins and uses.
Self-Defense: The famous "playing the dozens" in the ghetto is learning how to use language to deflect verbal harm and insults constantly coming at you from friends and the outer white world alike. The quick retort, the fast rejoinder was protection.

"This ability to defend against verbal jabs breeds a love of language too. A black youngster is constantly exposed to colorful, inventive ingenious language from all sectors of the culture: church, friends, media, and music all re-invent language constantly. There is no standard English other than what we speakers agree it is.

Language became a way to distinguish one's self and create a persona. You have sweet-talkers, ranters, professors, preachers, poets, musician or cool speak, slang, gang words, warnings against the police encoded in the language.
Language is power; it is entertainment on a Sunday afternoon—with no TV and no money for paid diversions. We all were entertaining one another armed with nothing the power to speak creatively. It is still that way. Listen on a ghetto

street corner and see what you hear. Rap music is the latest manifestation of a massive explosion of language. Obviate the drugs, treatment of women, but, underneath is a tremendous love of language and sound and the ability to move the listener to feel something.

That ability to move people is the test. Oratory is designed to motivate people, make them laugh, cry, get angry, or organize. That is the severe test the black speaker has, given the history of church preaching, where black ministers had shown the way. Black politicians had to learn to compete with that well-established speaking tradition to gain any success.

Obama learned that skill shaped it for a white middle class audience and it is widely acknowledged to be one of his strongest skills in the campaign.

But, underneath is another point to the rhetoric –that of establishing early on a personal connection with the audience, one that goes beyond one's political program. This personal connection can and does create a Teflon effect for Obama. Criticism of his policies, to many seemed beside the point. He was the point. And that is worth gold in politics.

These are the skills Obama acquired and they have their origins, at least in part, on the streets of Chicago.

Politics, Power and Authority:

Centrally, we then come to the question of what are the details of politics as practiced in Chicago and political lessons learned there by the young Obama. The long rap sheet against Chicago politics includes charges of corruption, machine politics, spoils practices, vote buying and selling, and behavior destructive of the body politic.

What you learn is sure, that is politics in Chicago. Politics, Chicago-Style, is the study of who gets what, when, where and how after the election. It is a spoils system about jobs, money, contracts, and influence peddling; politics influences virtually every facet of life in Chicago.

It decides whose garbage gets picked up and whose neighborhoods don't get garbage service on a regular basis; whose landlords are hauled into court for building violations and which ones don't; who gets the bad produce at the inflated price and who gets good, cheap produce; who gets the bad cops and no justice and who gets justice and no jail time; and who goes to jail for long terms; who gets adequate medical care and who gets no medical care at all; who gets the jobs handed out at city hall and who does not.

That is politics Chicago style. But, note it is a style the young Obama reacted to and fought against. Ethics policy and new ethical standards were among his first concerns as an Illinois senator and as President of the United States. He was not immune to it; he was tarnished by it, and to an extent, made concessions to it. But the mid-western moral streak his mother and grandparents gave him also made him react to it. He

fought against it, and did so in the first days of his presidency. The animus again lobbyists is part politics but also part moral. The mid-west has a strong moral streak and it plays a role here too. Obama has that moral streak.
So what about power? Power, in politics is gang-style power.

My gang is in control of the state house now, or city hall and you better go along to get along. Obama reacted to that notion of power and rejected it, fashioning empowerment as a model, as opposed to the power-as-spoils model. Besides, he realized that a true grass roots power model can beat the gang model. And he learned that, too, in Chicago; organizing Saul Alinsky style. Alinsky's model is common now--used by many organizations. But, it was born and perfected in Chicago. Obama absorbed its lessons and techniques.

Out of this come attitudes toward general authority as well. Is authority generally benign, or is authority corrupt? Is authority friendly to your needs or hostile to your needs? Does authority operate generally from moral precepts, like those blacks see and hear in their churches?
In a word no. Obama saw this too. He was to be the empowering authority.

Look at his cabinet choices, his push for bi-partisanship. These are not just random reactions and urges. They are deeply seated in Obama's psyche and embedded there as a young organizer to Chicago and as a politician learning how to win.

However, Obama views on organizing evolved. He finally read the fine print in the Alinsky organizing manual and came to understand that the real target of community organizing is not poor people. Poor people, generally, have little power and little influence in most communities. That is why their communities are neglected, and lack influence at city hall. No, the real target of community organizing is not the poor but the middle class. The middle class, mostly, white, have the real power and they must be activated to support change. This realization altered Obama's whole political approach. His message changed from a black-centered one to messages more acceptable to the while middle class-racial unity, the end of partisan politics, practical problem-solving. This was the route to political success and was consistent with both his personal inclinations, (having both white and black parents) his messages of hope, and having those messages be aimed at younger white college educated voters. Add to this those firm mid-western values I have spoken of, and we have Barack Obama presidential candidate. So the premise here is Obama's ideas, persona and precepts were forged in Chicago, in his family and both are value structures which were integral to the support he achieved in gaining the Presidency.

Character:

These traits all combined add up to character. Character is what we look for in a President and this President has a character, which we have above, identified. The sum of those traits is what we call character.

Strength, but with a sensitivity to things human, love of the land, of family; the ability to stand up when no one else agrees with your opinion, the ability to go out among neighbors and organize them, an understanding that if you make the first move people will notice and offer to help; as a sense that power is to be used for good; that morality always has a place and has its own rewards. And in all this, playing for keeps, not getting discouraged and maintaining the course. Add a bit of practically in politics and compromise when necessary to get to larger goals—you have, I believe Barack Obama.

As one of my uncle's stated. "Only you can get you out of bed each morning." And if you do that you can get others to do that too.

My view:

Character gives us the courage and the energy
to relentlessly press on
against impossible odds
and grow from adversity
and to develop the capacity for unconditional
Commitment.

Character is all we have
when we discover
we are all alone.

Growing Up
is simply acquiring
the courage and faith in one's self and others
and one's own Character to make the world a better
place than we found it.

This is the mid-western creed and I, Barack and others were
raised with its assumptions strengths and weaknesses.

The Mid-West--Chicago and Them:

I have interviews and notes from correspondents which are striking examples of those mid-western traits spoken about above. One comes from an Omaha woman, married to the same man for 30 years,
The steel determination in her letters, the iron resolve is illustrative of many mid-western attitudes.

Bitter Steel and Hard Love:

She was from the heartland and this striking statement of hers reflects the steely, pioneer, resolve characteristic of some mid-westerners. Descendents of the pioneers, these folks are bred to a hard tack, never-say-die determination.

This is reflected to in their personal relationships as well. Note here she loves her husband, but it is a bitter love which she has determined to un-do. Catherine is determined to un-love her husband!

Obama tapped into that steely determination and turned it into support. He is also counting on it to help to bring this nation back from the economic brink. But in looking at this, keep in mind that a President, especially Obama, changes how people look at themselves, their marriages, husbands, wives, and families.

I am phrasing her sentiments below.

Bitter-Tasting:
"I'm in between, bitter tasted; overcome by my own nature,
but, unrepented, I still am by choice and circumstance."

"I step upon my own fate plunge, holes in my own ship, live
with storms and tumult I alone create."

"I'm in between and bitter tasting overcome by my own
nature.
But, unrepented I still am by choice and circumstance."

"I've been wrong many times and humble enough to know, but
alone, I'm not strong enough to reverse trend, turn the bend
and came back again."

But, I still want to unlove you.
"Twirl me round one more time, whatever comes by me
will surprise; but, it will be mine.

I'm in between, bitters tasting; overcome by my own nature
but unrepented I still am by choice and circumstance.

My life complete will state in the Book of Summation:

Lived by Instinct; Died From Commitment: The Pallbearers
were Choice and Circumstance."
 I sent the above along to her to see if it captured her
sentiments and I asked what did wanting to "unlove" her
husband mean?

Interestingly, she tried to explain that she felt trapped in her relationship, in her life, and longed for something more, something different. But she was older, set in her ways and besides she loved her husband and her family.

But she was a stubborn woman, and strong. She also saw her love for her husband, indeed, her family as a weakness, which had ensnared her in a life she now regretted. She had wanted to be a ballerina, when she was young, but, the babies came. She had seen her ability to raise her family as strength, her ability to endure as strength, but now, in her later years, she began to doubt her strength. Maybe it was, in fact, a weakness. She was trapped, therefore, by both choice and circumstance.

But she would endure. And she did vote for Obama.
His family was from Kansas and that was good enough for her.

Character provides the courage to endure; hard times take extraordinary courage to endure and a steel spine. Many stories like these are being lived out every day in this country and around the world.

This summarizes how many respondents view their life situations and how they rely upon that hard resolve and determination to deal with every day life—an asset to Obama when they join his efforts and respond to his calls for American renewal.

An older gentleman said to me that "life is a slow motion mugging" but you get up, wipe the blood off and say: so?" "If you lose everything--rebuild, if you lose one arm team up with another one-arm man so between the two of you, you have two arms. You talk slow and you get up everyday and get the job done."

This kind of spirit is one forged in terrible winters, floods, storms, tornadoes and calamities; he said he had seen all his life. "Every time somebody predicts the end of the world they's wrong. The end of the world is when you die, meantime, there's work to be done."

He liked Obama, "young bright and ambitious. I like that," he said.

Goldilocks Is Not Afraid to Walk In The Woods:

Goldilocks is an internet nickname of a lady who exhibited a world view that said "I am not ceding the woods to the wolves. And, I am not taking any Tai-Bow classes either."

Goldilocks the fairy tale that stated that Goldilocks made the mistake of walking in the woods unwary of wolves; that her grandmother was eaten by the wolf.

This correspondent (age 14) was having none of that. She view was that she understood there was right and wrong, dos and don'ts—and rules; she didn't care. She was determined to live her own life as she saw fit. Restrictions, warnings that she would be sorry if she did not listen angered her. She saw the adult world as fearful, frail and incompetent in many respects. She felt confident in walking in the woods and was willing to rely upon her self to protect her self. She worked horses after school, feed them and cleaned the stalls. She took long rides by herself and felt most comfortable when "looking after her animals"

She had little respect for Goldilocks and lot of confidence in herself.

She liked Obama. She couldn't vote, but, thought it would be neat to have an African-American President.

This group of teens and pre-teens, I found, are not terribly political but, on the other hand, don't see race and color as much as their parents. They are riveted in the high school world which, for many of them, is a horrible experience. They

often include cutters, the meth-involved, the lonely, those feeling like outcasts, those angry, those bored and those bidding time to get out of the thousands of small towns they tend to live in.
They can't vote now, but that 14 year old just might-four years from now when Obama may run again.

Marriages and What to Do When There is no Cabbages:
Grandma's Advice on How to Make Your Marriage Work:

Marriages and relationships especially suffer when the economy goes bad, or war comes. This grandmother imparts her wisdom forged in the depression years.

She told her recently married daughter in law:
"Now you got married I need to tell you how to stay married. Marriages have not two people but three people in 'em. There's you, there him and there's the relationship. If you want to stay married don't all the time choose you; don't all the time choose him. Choose the relationship first. Don't want to end up in divorce court fighting over money and who didn't put the tooth paste cap back on.
Ain't worth it for your kids, ain't worth it putting our family though a divorce either.
You are expected to do you duty and stay together and raise a family. That's what it's all about. "

She liked Obama because his running put the image of the black family up a notch. She thought that was good for the black race and the white race too. Good to have a man who might be President upholding family things.
She closed by telling me she would never vote for Obama, but thought he was good for the black race.
But, aside from those Mid-westerners who supported him or

did not, who were the other Americans who identified with Obama and elected him, elevated him to the Presidency? Midwesterners did, Iowa Midwesterners did, but, what about the rest of America? What did they see in Obama?

Obama and the Professionals Classes:

The 18-35 year old, college-educated segments in America, worked hard for Obama, and are thought by some to be the key to his success. They were the generation he addressed early on; he organized them, inspired them and gained from them the financial and political support he needed to win. He continues to stay in contact with them via the internet.
He was one of them--the internet generation--used a blackberry, risked attempting a 3 point shot in front of the troops in Iraq--and made the shot, (talk about being an instant sports hero-every male in America understood what that shot meant-trying it and risking missing it. There went the troop vote, right over into Obama's column. That truly was the shot heard round the world.)

He talked openly about race in Philadelphia in a way that was acceptable and not blame-centered. He showed loyalty and devotion to his friend Rev. Wright; he was educated and not afraid to introduce thoughtful action into the political dialogue. He did not seem to hate whites or reject them as human beings or demonize them. He loved his grandmother. He contrasted himself with McCain who came across in the financial crunch looking like George Bush: all action and no plan. All of this had strong appeal to the professionals and the college-educated.

This group loved Obama, and, I think, and are still an important source of support, are still connected to him-- naturally via the internet.

Who are they? They are the civil-libertarians, college students, the American Civil Liberties Union, Move On, org, the young

and restless, the "sick of the republicans group", the small business people who saw their lives falling apart, the rust belt small town professionals who thought—why not give the black guy a shot, the generational rebels who looked at grandma and grandpa and asked who made this mess you're leaving us with? And white professionals who saw in him a professional like themselves.
A few of their stories:

The Doctor Is In:

He is the English major who became a doctor at a major medical institution in California and forsook his first love--writing. In between patients he continued to write, and read one of my earlier books. He is playful, played with writing, and, he loved the English language.

Dr. X strongly supports Obama and his proposal to computerize medical records and his institution has already computerized many of its medical records. Dr. X works with a computer on his lap while seeing patients.

Doctoring, he thinks, is under siege—from hospitals who gain the profits while he performs the services, from patients who don't understand how little the state and federal government pays for their services, from the drug companies who have brought off the politicians, from the media who put commentators on the screen who are being paid by those same drug companies; politicians who gouge on donations from those same drug companies and media conglomerates, from reporters whose papers are owned by the same conglomerate groups.

"As a doctor, I am the owner of a small business with maybe three employees. I am not Mercy General. I am a small business person surrounded by the conglomerates that gouge me and there is little I can do about it."

Big government taking over health care? So what would change? He is not sure, but, he likes the idea that Obama might make his job easier. The charting process would be taken out of the hands of some nurses who don't fill the charts in correctly, who's hand-writing can be a challenge. Dr. X likes the Obama persona. He is a professional, thoughtful person. The nurse at his office agreed "Sure it is a good idea because many medical errors are due to the fact that clear handwriting is not taught in medical school. "So computerize," she thought, "it would make her job easier."

Doctors generally have not supported wholesale reform of the Health Delivery system in the United States. That, however, may be changing as doctors have begun to feel like cogs in the health conglomerate chain.

Nurses feel the pinch too. While many don't like doctors, (nurses do all the work, doctors get all the pay is their mantra) nurses too, feel overworked by a system where one nurse may have to care for 15-20 patients. Given the nurse shortage, nurses welcome any way to make the job easier.

Our doctor's nurse told me nurse jokes about doctors. Here's one. A long line of people are waiting to get into heaven, and, one person, a doctor in operating blues, jumps the line and goes past every one. A person in line asks why the doctor is able to jump the line ahead of us."
"Oh" St. Peter says "that is God, he likes to dress up like a doctor."

Nurses, I know, since I worked organizing them in San Francisco, are finishers--exhibiting a brand of devotion to their patients that mid-westerners find familiar. Nurses see themselves as there at birth, there at death and the real work-horses of the medical profession. It's true, and everyone seems to agree, nurses run hospitals. The life and death drama that hospitals are--is familiar to nurses--many, of whom are from rural areas and comfortable with the life cycle.

They also make better than average incomes and have more job flexibility than most professions. The scarcity of nurses in the United States has made the trained nurse much in demand. The ones I talked to liked Obama. Those mid-western values he displayed were familiar to them. I am sure many didn't vote for him, but, I think the generalization that most did is true. Their thought is that anything that fixes what is wrong with doctors is a good thing. Their issues with doctors: God complex, bad hand-writing, and, being overpaid.
Obama might just fix two of the three.

The Berkeley Lawyer Power Couple:
(Let's Not Kill All The Attorneys—We are Two of the Good Ones)

They are the Berkeley two, lawyers both. Obama's election was history come to roost, time turning back slavery, vindication of the Civil War; the rejection of the lynching period in American history, the restoration of civil liberties gutted by the Bush Administration; and, now, Obama had an opportunity to right those wrongs-to bring America back together after the long Republican night of division and acrimony. Obama was joining the country in a new consensus where healing was possible.

Time froze election night. They wept at his victory. America had stepped up and had done the right thing in electing him— rejecting the distorted and destructive policies George Bush and the Cowboy ethic of the past eight years had stood for. They felt like battered children, having lived in an abused family and finally, the relatives, or social services had knocked on the door and they were to be released from the control of the evil step parent.

The over-whelming sense of relief, of joy, of pride in country were all in this mix.
Now whether this view will or will not prove to be accurate in the long run does not matter, I believe that The Moment--when the networks announced he had won--was a tremendous unifying moment for all the world, whites, blacks, Asians, Latinos, Europeans, Kenyan's, even the French. Oprah cried, Jessie Jackson cried, people cried in living rooms all across America-- dried tears on the sofa cushions--for days later.

Calls went out all over the world—"did you hear? He won. He won."

The planet has few moments of that feeling of being part of a world community--this was one, this was an indelible vision, which is, and was historic?
Hope took a bow. Hope for the end of silly, politically driven divisions and that a multi-cultural, post racial America could gain some hold on the future; that trillions spent on war could be spent on peace and re-building America.
Still, as one pundit put it: Maybe nothing at all will change and all we have done is to give the Black Guy the worse job in the world.

Whether this turns out to be the case depends in part on events, (who can control events?) and Barack Obama's own skills. However, it also depends upon professionals like these two. They believe, they donate significant sums of money, they are the actives who, if they succumb to disillusionment, and disappointment, and, if in doing so, return to private life and apathy, the Obama dream is also likely up for failure.

Their children, fifty-percent of whom return home after college, have no jobs in sight, are the shock troop organizers of Obama's next phase--re-election. If they are the troopers, these professional parents are the financiers who will give these not-working young people the support they will need to work on their own future and Obama's. They volunteer in his army, take part in programs aimed at them. Social security, buying a home of their own, marriage, war, children—all these are the future the children contemplate and Obama is their leader.

The African-American Professional and Non-Professional Reactions:

The African-American Middle Class, of course, supported Obama, worked for Obama, cried when he won, but, the African-American community has its divisions too. Was he black enough, was he too white, did his white background ruin him for understanding urban blacks and their problems; did growing up in Hawaii really give him a sense of southern blacks and their problems?
Long-established African-American leaders eyed him warily at first. He was the new kid the block. Should they be pushed aside for him?

Jackson made some unfortunate off camera remarks, some black leaders sat on their hands for much of the early campaign.

The hip-hop music industry dominated by African-American talent was different. They embraced Obama from the start. "Will I Am" from the Black-Eyed Peas worked for Obama, wrote for Obama, sang with a multi-racial group and spent money, raised money to get out the vote. They sang. danced and played for him.

But, the group which gave its heart to Obama was the middle and the less than middle-class; the black single mothers in the Northern cities, the Black single and married women in the south, The beauty-polar vote, the barber shop vote, the church vote, the urban black voters, turned out, as we know, 90-95 percent for Obama.
So why?

He was black, but, there had been blacks running for President before. They did not get that kind of support, certainly not that kind of adulation. So what gives here?
Let's focus on Hope, for a moment--that was Obama's message.

Here is one difference between Obama's run and those runs for President conducted by other black leaders-- spoken to me by one black mother.

"If you listen to some black leaders they tell you that we are the last hired and first fired and poor and poor again for generations, and that is the fault of the white man. But there ain't no hope in that statement. It don't tell me how I am going to pay the bills and feed the kids."

"Barack says he'll help. He will be in control and he'll help. And besides it dawns on you watching mother's scream and yell at their kids, slapping them around in the supermarket, that that mother is not raising no freedom fighter, she is raising a resentful kid who get a gun some day and shoot somebody—likely my kid."

"Got to move beyond all that, like Obama says, don't hit 'um-- read to "um."

But whites, especially poor whites, had their view as well. They had much in common with just below-middle-class blacks. They, too, saw hope in what Obama was saying. This is Maggie.

Maggie's Story:
The First Shall Be Last:
She was the ugly duckling, the last of seven children who fell in love with the high school football star who never gave her a second glance. She mentioned that she felt like Quasimodo at fourteen and an outcast.

Obama was to be her salvation, the vindication of her life-long belief that devotion in the long run outdistances the hare in the race while Pretty is still on the side line powering its pretty face.
"The last shall be the first," she said. "my still-borns" (there were two) "shall not be in vain. Their remains are my monuments. Love has no price, even beyond death.

This story touched me. For many, they are Quasimodo and Obama is a reflection of their faith that wrongs will be righted for the devoted and Obama represents to them, I think, an vision of themselves.

She represents a large number American blacks and whites who clearly heard Obama promise that the "First shall be Last and the Last shall be Elevated" in recognition of their devotion and they, in this the "Now Time," will be given their just due. Many, many single mothers see themselves as willing to lay down their lives for their children and their families. That is as huge a love as Quasimodo had.

Quasimodo lived the church tower, penniless, ugly, repelled and he loved Esmeralda, a hopeless love, doomed. He died, but, his story lives on because of the magnitude of his love.

For families, especially women, in raising children, their entire life- force is aimed at not only raising their kids and supporting the family, they see, some of them, as their sacrifice, as their life's work. Their memory will be passed down the generations. Families are a kind of monument to their love and caring. A piece on Quasimodo (Love's Remains) really resonated with this group and they wrote to me about it.

That sounds a bit old fashioned, but, its there in the letters and writings.

You cannot help, but, see that for some African-American women Obama represents to them the ideal African-American family-now raised up for the whole world to see, to counter the images of the black decimated family-he vindicates their countless urgings to their own children that education matters.

"See what Barack did?" they tell their children. Obama is an emotional icon too, the strong family-oriented black man, while, they, many of them, have no male in the house to help raise the kids.

Now they do.

They too suffer from the media stereo-types depicting black women as hostile, abrasive and not pretty compared to white women. Difficult topic here but true. Skin color matters in America and around the world. The more similar individuals in the colonized group look to the colonizer they gain status are given more support by colonized and the colonizers alike.

From this circumstance black women have adopted responses that say, if I am not to be chosen, then I will go it alone, put all my love into my family, if I am not to be chosen then they will know my anger and my rejection; not chosen then I will find love in my church or more recently in work.

Obama raises them up in their minds. The belief that their child can get a good education and become President of the United States is stunningly vindicated for them who placed all their love and devotion into their children, telling them they can succeed with education; the ugly tortoise wins the race while the Pretty Hare sits on the sideline powdering its pretty face.

The Slacker Generation and the Unfocussed:

Aroused by Obama's candidacy, millions of younger
Americans gained from Obama' a sense of focus and purpose.
A story of what I call "The Slacker Two."

The Slacker Two:
They were the Slacker Generation feeling sidelined by history
until Obama came. His story was their story. His way became
their way. His future became their future.
Before this, this couple saw themselves mired in flat-lined lives;
"self absorbed pronouns" with no direction forward. He gave
hints. He gave direction and "the slacks moved from similes to
nouns."

(The thoughts of a 19 year old voting for the first time.)
John was an English major thinking in English-major terms.
Out of his correspondence came one of my best inspirations for
connecting the structure of the English language with the mood
of a country, of a generation expressed in the parts of speech
dominant in the language. "Simile" to me, describes the mood
of that generation, in its own language terms.

Feel Like a Simile Sometimes

"I feel like a train sometimes that can't get no locomotin,'
my wheels lumber and my Ideals get stuck in sideways roller
motions. I feel like the moon sometimes beautiful but dead.

Feel like thinking sometimes but get tangled up in emotions. Feel like a bird sometimes remembering how to soar. Feel like sleeping sometimes and not getting up, being in bed for a while. Feel like Christmas when someone gives me a smile. Feel like feeling more on certain days and times. Feel like talking deep and thinking light-laughing loud and quiet.
Feel like feeling like my best days sometimes. Feel like is feeling like if life rhymes sometimes. Feel like is feeling like if the rhythm beats in time, if my heart skips to music quips and rejoins at the metered line. Feel like is feeling like feeling is ok; but feeling good or bad without that like is better; well... Like superior. Like ok?"

Here, even in the final thoughts in this piece, there is ambiguity because getting away from feeling like a simile in today's world is not easy.

While Obama gave this group purpose and direction--thought of him as cool, and, one of them, they are the generation with a truncated future, no social security, endless war, without affordable housing. Many live five to a house or apartment, no jobs or are under-employed—having known only a political system many of them associated with Republicans and George Bush--careers shaky, parental support waning—the parents are not retiring , blocking growth paths for the young.
This generation understands that Obama has no magic bullet; they see that real answers are not likely to come from any one. They have stepped up to help but, deep down just don't see what they can do. Their life circumstances don't look like they will change.

Marriage is postponed, marriage age is rising. Who can afford a family, or even a house? Child-bearing is down, or postponed because children are expensive, and who would bring a child into this world except the wealthy, the selfish or the foolish? So in the face of massive adult failures, failures to stop George Bush, failures to save the environment, failure to stop jobs from going overseas, failure to leave anything behind for them except a wasteland of mounting problems; they think why not give one of them a chance at ultimate power. At least Obama is one of them. This is an interesting group in that I got the feeling that they live in small groups, with room-mates, date in groups, party in groups, they don't see themselves, some of them as fully grown adults, even past age thirty. Men and women play video games for hours upon hours. Relationships are described to me, sounding like individuals, even those living together as a couple, have the feel of brother and sister, not real adults ready to act in the world. The world acts upon you, you don't act upon the world. They tend to be fascinated by their parents stories of sixties activists. That generation to the slackers seemed to be a generation that went to the streets. This group does not go to the streets. They volunteer, but they don't riot.

So, we have a group that will respond to something like National Service. That is a group activity they can resonate with. Obama is offering something that makes sense to them, plus help with college tuition.

Meantime, marketers market to them continuing to make cartoon and comic books hero movies, because this group often lives in the virtual world as much as the real one. This is prolonged child-hood, never felt quite like an adult generation—"living in my parent's basement group."

Humm, who is a real life hero--Superman gone to Washington? That thought had appeal to many in this group and they voted for Obama.

The Suburbanites and the Down-Unders:

This is a group I am very familiar with. We are the homeowners living close by a big city; college-educated, bought the house and now sit in those houses, now worth less than what we paid for them-many in foreclosure.
We are the group with worked hard, got an education, pursued the American dream ran into the brick wall of wall street greed, whose life savings dropped by half in less that a year, who sit simmering on the edge of anger, unable to see the next year, unable to peer into a future which grows dim.

We know Obama will not be able to fix it all, and even if he does, there will be a price, inflation, jobs continuing to flee, our children having a huge debt to pay off. Not a good choice in sight here.

Our children are the first in American history who cannot look forward with any certainty to a future better than their parents had, to a better, bigger house, a better job, a bigger bank account, These educated children of the educated middle class are at home living in the basement, or off in a city somewhere else leading an iconoclastic life backed up by these parents with credit cards, money and support.
One father, a friend of mine, described to me what his son, living in New York was doing with his life so far:

"He called me and told me that he was part of a group called 'The Roving Band of Lovers."
The Roving Band of Lovers, it turned out was a street theater group which C. described as "going around lifting people's spirits, singing in the subways, doing street plays and being kind to people"

To him this was a waste of time and would not lead his highly educated son to anything what would be productive.

"He kisses little old ladies hands, dress up like a 16th century courtier and smiles at people. He sent his mother and I a Satin Valentine Heart. These he hands out to people who need love in their lives, he says."

"We are of course worried about him. What is he doing with his life?"

Becky, the daughter of another friend was described to me from a conversation she had with a friend of Becky's. The mother didn't recognize her daughter in the friend's description. The friend said "Becky is wonderful; she wears pirate stripe shirts, and little black boots. She goes into restaurants and asks each table what is good to eat and asks for samples of what they are eating. She doesn't take tuition classes anymore. She audits her classes and spends the money on acting lessons. She goes to the best hotels, showers, and uses the spas and the swimming pools without registering. She holds pot-luck dinners in her apartment building where people come and tell the story of how they dumped in the last relationship. She goes to weddings uninvited, says she is the photographer, eats and leaves. She reads the obituaries, goes to wakes or funerals, weeps, eats and leaves. She brought a cheap take-recorder and interviews wealthy or powerful people to make contacts.

Of course, this is not reassuring to these middle class parents. Their kids, some of them, seem adrift.

However, that dry middle class sense of humor is still there however, it is a bit darker; but still there. Here are a few precious bits of overheard conversations I have heard or was told to me at parties.

"I not really fat' he said 'I am anorexic, just not very good at it."

"So I told her it was ok she could sleep with him, but, she would have to pay for that pair of shoes we saw at Nordstrom's."

"So my Dad says 'All I am asking for is a Some Sex Marriage.'

"So he says he is not gay he just likes men."

"I threw up on him and he was so sweet, he wiped it off and I tipped him a dollar."

"And then I found out that the tattoo he put on my butt was his ex-girl friend."

"Girl he is ugly no way around the facts unless you saying he is packing."

"She stood there and let all the men get a good look at her cleavage. How can you compete with that?"

"I don't really read books and stuff like that takes too long."

"I told him he never listens to me and he said 'What?'

"I don't know, the honey moon was a disaster-we made love for only about five hours and he started complaining about his back."

"What's your name again? You got a girlfriend? Yes, she said."

"So he heard us making love on the answering machine--the thing was on room monitor."

"I told him the baby was his, but, of course, there was no baby."

"So he said 'You are bleeding is that normal? 'Normal' I said bleeding? And then I passed out."

"Well he is very tall, got big feet, a big nose. and bedroom eyes; all the things I need in a man right now."
"I had to set him free. Hard to be with a man prettier than you." "We really like Obama; he's not really black you know."

But, despite the humor, serious questions face the middle class and their off-spring.
Has, the American dream crash-landed in the open field; is the gathering power of other countries-clearly evident now, threatening to move the America we know to the status of a third-world debtor- nation mired in hopeless debt?

Are we, in the so-called "first world" seeing the juggernaut of demographics over take Europe, the Italians, the English, the French, the Russians, all countries with such low birth rates that in 40 years there will be no more of these historic cultural entities. They will likely be replaced by high birth populations from the South, Muslims, Algerians, Africans, Middle-Easterners—all forming the cheap labor pool now but destined to gradually replace their employer populations in fifty years. In the United States, it is the Mexican-American birth rate which outstrips the American birth rates. Demographics is destiny.

If the population doesn't get you, the environment, food and water shortages, financial failure looms disease, virus threats, all loom on the landscape. The American educated classes now are understanding this and know there is no solution currently in hand,

But is it all bleak? Bleak to be sure. But impossible to overcome? No. While there is no widespread realization yet, there is the growing consensus among this group that the consumption society is over. No more can 2% of the world's population consume 25% of its goods and services.

This group understands that and has cut back on its consumption but consternated by the exhortation that cutting back on consumption can make this worse. Conundrum. What is true here?

This group has decided to cut back, and not increase buying. That decision, if held to, will revolutionize American society and force its reorganization. More on that later.
But the summary point is clear: So goes the American, educated middle class—so goes America.

The Environmentalists
The Heart-Land Engineer and the Water Supply:

He is the engineer who had been reading about heart-land
cities selling their water rights away to the highest bidder. Air
rights and mineral rights were on the auction block too.
Rust belt cities were selling out the tax base to the Wal-Mart's
of the world reducing the tax base which could not then
support the new sidewalks needed, the sewer repairs; the
highway repairs. The young people were moving away, the
houses and the houses were falling apart. He was the engineer
at the filtration plant watching the Aquifer cry. He is alarmed
that half of water in this country is wasted by out-date water
mains which burst and spill precious drops.

He is encouraged by the Obama administration's talk of
creating a national energy grid, of infrastructure
improvements and support for the industrial base.
He pointed out to me that water tables and aquifers were being
destroyed or damaged through out the world.

Ecological damage meant poisoned ground water which ran
into the streams, endangering the lives of those that depend
upon that water, increasing the costs of cleaning and filtrating
the poisoning agents out.

"Water" he said, was" the well-source of all civilization,"
sustained early man, made life possible even in the desert. The
Earth is two-thirds water he constantly noted.
"As the water table goes," he said, "we go."

He believed that life on Earth began in the sulphur of hot-springs, like those found in Yellow Stone park. The Earth it self gave birth to life. Water is our life-blood and we risk all by not dealing with the water issues in this country.

He does not see any immediate solutions. Making sea-water drinkable, after the salt is removed, is a possibility, but, the process is extremely expensive and would likely be privately owned. Some countries are trying it, like Dubai, but they are small countries and have plenty of capital to expend. A project in the United States could cost trillions we don't have.
What to do? What to do?

He, I imagine, would strongly support Obama's new stimulus package. It looks like some of it is aimed at projects that, he as an engineer, would approve. But underneath his discussion is the conviction, I believe, that the trillions dollars it would take to repair the infra-structure of this country, infrastructure long neglected, will not happen in the Obama administration, or any administration--just not the will or the money to get it done.

Where are we going? "We will have a bridge or two collapse and some hurry-up-fix-it-stuff, but, nothing will really change. We are headed for third-world conditions in this country, things break and they won't get fixed."

He has some hope for green technology but not much— excepting if it goes toward protecting the water supply. But, that will cost and we, in this country, don't have the money. He sees the Chinese buying up whole towns and maybe even the great lakes going up for sale.

The Indian Mother:

He is an American Indian and the Earth Mother image is part
of his religion. "The Mother which nourishes us" he said, takes
care of us makes all life possible for us. You don't stick knives
in your mothers' belly; you don't poison your mother's food.
You don't drink your mother's life-blood."
Thanks to him for making me understand that the Earth
Mother is family.
This perspective on the environment is not, of course,
unfamiliar but, I have found that younger people have an
especially emotional response to the environmental issue
expressed in familial terms. This mirrors my American Indian
friends view as well.
Here is an example of a poem which drew strong emotional
response from young people, especially teens.

The Earth Speaks

"I am the Earth, your mother;
you are my children.

I am
the cosmic dust
of a thousand, billion, trillion stars;
conceived in tumult,
I've endured millions of asteroid hits
and cataclysmic comet shots.

Hot lava flowed over my face,
volcanic steam;
my body seethed
for millions of years;

titanic explosions
blew out my insides;
where time and time again,
asteroids destroyed all my life;
but, I started again;
renewed it.
Relentless,
I have created
blue oceans;
continents, and wood greens,
and life, life
everywhere.

I took from the seas
my tiniest amino
bits
and created life;
one cell first,
then colonies
then whole beings,
you;

I nurtured these small creatures,

your sisters and brothers.

I gave you the moon
for silver nights,
the stars for inspiration--
a magnetic shield
to protect you from the burning rays of the sun;

I gave you food, trees and animals

so that you might thrive.

You are all my children
whom I have given a world of plenty
reared you in Paradise.

I took you from the caves--
showed you fire--
sacrificed my own wood trees--
so that you might eat your food--
gave you animal skins
of my own creations--
to shelter you from wily winds.

Gave you water.

I showed you the beauty of the stars
and, too, alas,
a brain big enough to study war.

And you did discover war;
you discovered hate;

you took my abundance
and despoiled it.

My forests now burn
ignited by your hand;
you have rent my face with mining scars
and quarries;
polluted my rivers and oceans
for beads and baubles;
for fleeting shiny things

for your amusements;
and then you threw them away;
whole pollution mountains you've created.

There seems no retreat from you
and the relentlessness
with which you pursue
all this
for reasons
I do not fathom;
my thin, thin, crust ages.

Hear me my children;
my fate is entrapped
with yours,
whether you live
is whether I live;

what you do
can destroy my oceans
and life itself.

I will return to being a cold rocky world
in the rushing void;
my blues
will become grey
and then black.

Hear me my children
for we are family."

This part of the environmental movement, teens, new age adults, and old-style conservationists draw the lesson that indeed, like our mid-westerners, the land is the source of all we have on the planet, is the source of our wealth. It is our Mother.

Younger people mention in their letters that environmental themes are taught in schools and they read about it and have a personal feel for the environment many adults have lost or never had.

But, ask a mid-westerner, ask my grandfather, ask my great grandfather, ask most of the immigrants to this country and they will tell you that land, having your own plot of land is integral to the American dream and the American promise.

That dream Barack Obama, seems to understand, is in danger of slipping away according to many of them. They understand that he understands and they voted for him.

But, among younger teens the sentiments in this poem has emotional impact based on their having seen their real mothers cry at home, for abuse, or divorce or troubled times. They can see themselves as a child version of mother earth, or their grand mother. The environment is not just the physical environment but the emotional environment of their every-day lives.

The Environmentalist Anthropologist: Gene Pool Too Small:

The anthropologist wrote to say that research money was needed to do gene pool tracings from that period in human history where climate had decimated the human race down to about 14 thousand human beings.

His point was that, this was a too small a gene pool that we humans are descended from-- not large enough to support healthy gene pool development; that human behavior, erratic, warlike, peaceful, building, and destructive are contradictory behaviors; and schizophrenic. He wanted Obama to provide money for that research for genetic research, which he thought could potentially clarify the genetic issues surrounding the schizophrenic nature of human nature.

Smart Apes

The trees are leaving;
lurched away;
heading magnetic north;
sap cooled
and cold.

The elms
uproot themselves;
and go.

Shade is gone.
The house is warm less;
night prolonged.

I see birds laboring west

unclear and direction-less.

Nature's abandonment
is profound.

I see no humming bird
at the outside feeder
now for weeks.
A tragedy.

Sorrow is a hoof-less stag,
the stunted bud on the flowerless tree,
the wind that weeps.

The bad air is Grey Green

'Beware of Smart Apes
wielding intelligence
uncontrolled.

Hope is the mutancy
which may overcome
Smart Ape genetic Mutancies;

Personal Stories during Obama's Run For the Presidency:

However much American's class groupings reacted to Obama's candidacy, much of the Obama saga was revealed to me in terms of what was going on in the personal lives of respondents over the two year period of his run for the Presidency. These are personal stories related to Obama's long protracted run for the Presidency.
Here are a few:

Obama's Soul Kiss:

 She discovered kissing at fourteen, and, her writing was full of its joys. Her first kiss was Obama in Iowa--during his Iowa victory speech. She sat on the couch with her boyfriend awed by that speech as many were across the world... A black man had won in an all-white state and gave what is now regarded one of the most generation-inspiring speeches of all time.
It felt new, it was new; it was a new President in the making and people could feel it.

 It was her first soul-kiss and perhaps the first soul kiss for the nation.

 The soul kiss Mary K. described parallels the soul kiss of a nation experiencing its first contact with a potential African-American President; the fist-bump, welling tears, blacks and whites, race in America, the right and the left wing all in the mix—all of the American cultural agonies spilling out onto the table. Barack Obama was the catalyst—a first kiss from a multi-racial President and America liked it-a lot. So did Mary K. She read my piece and wrote me about her first soul kiss. It was a reaching out letter, a young person saying "I can relate to a black man" I got myself a soul kiss. And what soul kiss it apparently was. (A soul kiss is where in the act of kissing, months closed, the two individuals exchange breaths back and forth. The effect is euphoric and dizzying.)

But a kiss is still a kiss; it is not a successful courtship and may or may not lead to any permanent enduring relationship.

History tells us that again and again we Americans think we have solved one or more of our enduring problems, war, race, prosperity, love and hate, and we learn nothing is permanent. Things change but these same problems re-surface again and again.

But for now that first soul kiss in Iowa remains sweet. Nothing can take that one back and it lives in Mary K's memory and in the memory of a nation.

Months later, I checked in on the soul kiss. "Still sweet" she said.

Long Gone, Obama's on the TV:

While all the world held its breath waiting for results on election night he left her with two kids and no money. She watched TV while he took the pick-up truck and their few things, leaving her watching Obama on the TV. While much the world chose to celebrate, she had no one. Her hand presses keys on the computer and her anguish comes through.

Her life in her small town was falling apart. Her live-in boy-friend left her with little or no means. She needed hope and for the first time in her life she started to pay attention to politics. She started to listen to Obama and began that slow process of placing her Hope Basket at his door, tried to see what he was offering, what future could he assure her was possible for her where she lived.

She had listened to Hillary but Hillary was offering her a "you go girl" which rang hollow. She needed help and she needed help soon.

She liked the gas tax holiday. Every penny counted. She wanted a gas tax holiday, but it didn't' happen and she was disappointed that it did not happen. She looked at McCain. He was old. Let's face it. He was old and she didn't think he would survive the Presidency or be around for a second term. So there was Obama. Most of the men in her life had failed her. All the men in her life had been white men making promises. Now she had nothing.

She talked about her situation with two of her best friends. They helped her with loans and baby-sitting and that was good. But when she talked about voting for Obama there was a silence from both of them. She waited to see what each would say. Joyce's first comment was "gosh, I had a dream about him too." Joyce thought Helen was talking about a dream about voting for Obama. Helen told her "no. not a dream, for real."

"For real? Joyce said. Helen said "For real." Joyce's next response was "Did you see that naked picture of him in the water." That was a good looking man. You really are going to vote for him?"
"Think so." Joyce said.

Marge was wary. "People find out you voted for the black man and you might as well pack your things and leave town. You know how people talk. Grace will know, she looks at how everyone votes. They ought to do something about that woman. Registrar, my butt, she is a gossip."

Helen, stuck to her determination to vote anyway she wanted to and gradually, Joyce and Marge came around and decided to vote for Obama too. It took courage, in a small town, to expose yourself like that. Last report, I got, was that it wasn't so bad. Turns out the mayor announced he was voting for Obama too—the town might get some money from the Feds.

This is a compilation story but typical of many I received. It was an act of courage in some small towns, and even families to be public about voting for the black guy. It went against, traditions long in place in some communities, often placed you up against family members, church members; it might even affect your job.

It was as well no small thing to go further and make phone calls for the candidate.

Now in some circumstances, Obama's college students and young people showed up and knocked on your door. You could talk to them and they identified ways to get involved by making phone unobtrusively to voters in other cities. But most often if a candidate came to town, people like Joyce would go and sit in the back and listen. If Obama came to a near-by city where no one knew her, she would go take pictures and try to shake his hand.

At some point, small town or not, the growing feeling emerged that this election was different. People, like Joyce saw the English, the Germans, all whites, celebrating him, adoring him. It made her feel that her small town bigots were the ones out of touch and somehow it made it easier to cast her vote.

Jealousy, Election Week and Obama:

She said "I couldn't talk to him about my ex. His jealousy went to rage in short shrift. I was afraid."

"I smothered my feelings, and, made secret calls to my old boyfriend to ask what to do. How to deal with this. He was so kind. I missed him."

She was discovered on the phone to the ex. The phone bills confirmed all suspicions. She felt like a hostage unable to leave, but can't stand living there. It didn't help that the ex boy friend was Nigerian.

She like most in her town publically stated she said she would never vote for a black man. She never had. But, she had a black boy friend once, a sweet guy from Nigeria, who had attended the local college. She got along real well with him. Obama's mother had a black boy friend and husband from Kenya. The parallel was striking to her.

Her Nigerian boy friend showed her a different culture. Nigerians at the local college held parties all the time, laughed, had a good time and had English accents. She slipped away with her best friend and went to the parties. They were treated like queens. She was swept up with Abel and the romance lasted for six months.

She was criticized, she got the looks, and she knew that her old friends and her old group would never take her back. Her grandmother and her mother not so much, but, most of the rest of her family thought she had lost her mind.

The affair ended and she met Billy and they took up three years later. Billy had recently moved to her town- "all wild and full of confidence" was her description.

Billy found out about Abel. He saw the phone bill to Nigeria and hit the roof over the cost. Someone told him about Abel. Billy had a temper. He invented problems to complain about in the relationship
and withdrew. It didn't help that he couldn't find work and left her.

Obama came on the television. After that she did volunteer work for him, making phone calls to another city.

She and Abel have taken to corresponding and talking by email. He is very interested in keeping up with how Obama is doing and what he is doing. She thinks he might return to the United States at some point, but she is not sure.

They do not have a romance going or anything like that. Just friends.

But she is taken with Obama. She watches him, keeps up on the news and feels like his future and her future are all tied up together.

Love and Rejection-Obama Did It:

She said he was a difficult man, demanding, yet docile when she challenged him. He seemed to wilt and purr under her critical gaze; she told him that he was her second choice; that she could have done better. He seemed to like her more the more critical of him she became. He seemed most comfortable when she told him he was not worthy. She had a crush on Obama because he didn't seem to be like that. She voted for him, but, no one she knew did--and she didn't tell.
But her boyfriend knew she had a crush on Obama. He considered it, she thought, a further rejection of him. But, it also seemed to excite him. He would quiz her about the crush, wanted to know what it was about Obama that she liked. He wanted details. He began to ask for almost daily reports. It moved from Iowa, intensified in New Hampshire, and was agony in Pennsylvania and the ugly summer when things were going bad.

Obama became involved her personal relationship. She went to see him when he came to town near her. She shook his hand. He didn't know her, of course, didn't know who she was at all. Her boyfriend waited for her in the pick-up and didn't say anything about it on the way home. She wrote him a letter afterward, but only a form letter back.

She follows what he is doing. For her, I am thinking, Obama has the aura of a soap opera lover—handsome, trustworthy, who is always there. To her, he is someone she could see on the television every day. She devoured the tabloid news about him. She wanted details on his life with Michelle.

She followed Oprah's odyssey with him. Oprah fell in love with Obama, that was obvious. Oprah was among many women in America who fell in love with Obama. She cried on election night, she cried the tears of not just happiness for someone she campaigned for. No those tears were the sparkle kind, the kind a woman in love cries when the one she loves does good.

Women every where knew Oprah, knew her every facial expression from 15 years of watching her on television. Oprah did have a man, but Steadman was long gone. Oprah had a new man now and she couldn't hide her tearful tears of joy. New Hampshire Down:

She fell in love in New Hampshire when he lost, she felt it: the loss touched her, connecting her with the political world for the first time. But, it opened up her heart, too, and softened it such that her boyfriend became her finance after he saw her crying in front of the TV set.

For years she had been telling him "no" to marriage, didn't want to get stuck in a small town; but, that night her heart door was open and the boy-friend walked right in.

It was life-changing moment. It is strange to explain. Rodney understood her feelings about Obama, but, took it much in the way that she was into soap opera characters on television. He didn't mind her daily reports on what was happening in the campaign. He seemed genuinely interested in Obama. Election week was electric and election night, they sat together with her kids, from her ex and they cried too. She jumped up and down, the kids were screaming. He had won.

It was like they all had a hand in making it happen by praying for it.

She watches the news every day since the election. She loves the Obama family, especially the girls. She says she is looking forward to watching them grow up on the White House. Obama has become a part of her family, Her kids love the Jonas Brothers, and Obama's kids like the Jonas Brothers. She and her current fiancé fell in love election night and Obama was there. They, like others are struggling and Obama is on the television every day trying to help. They could see him, hear him. He seemed to care and he worked hard. The man worked hard.

All that is reassuring to both of them.

Sandy and the Black-Eyed Peas:

"I fell in love with him, from his speech at the democratic convention, I watched and cried. The Black-Eyed Peas sang. From the campaign trail I lived and died every set-back, triumph and trial."

"He became that part of me that pressed down hard on feeling hope again. Doesn't matter what the man does, and, does not achieve; somehow just his being there is good enough, for now, for me."

The song "I've Got A Crush On Obama" described the feelings of many of the electorate, especially women. Many did have a crush on Obama. And it showed. He shot to rock star status and remains there.

But why? Why Obama? There is, I believe, an emotional current to that adulation. Obama affects people emotionally. That is what a good orator does. That is what a good political speaker does. But what are those emotions?

The first was his electrifying speech and the 2004 Democratic Convention—which is when most Americans became aware of him. No one had heard him speak before, except the Illinois electorate. But there he was on national television, looking, stick-skinny but boy could he deliver a speech.

"There are no red states, there are no blue states, and there is only the United States."

For a country yearning for internal piece this was an electrifying message putting into words what many felt, but could not articulate. Barack did articulate that feeling. Liberals got excited. He was at once taking back the patriotism issue, the racial divide and wedge issues the Republican's had feasted on for years and was re-capturing Fort Sumner. He took back the American dream and showed to Americans who felt that it was been neglected, thrown aside in the closet during the Republican era.

For many it was good enough to elect him President. Just to have him there for four or eight years re=affirming those American values was enough. Forget, Rev. Wright, forget qualifications and years of experience,--what had those years of experience done for the country—not much.

It doesn't get any better than when people vote for you based on who you are, not your qualifications, not your policies, not even your programs. They voted for Obama the man, period.

And he was cute, dynamic, a good speaker and someone who might help America re-gain some of its lost luster overseas. All this could be accomplished with the simple act of voting. People made up their minds early and largely did not change. McCain tried everything. Nothing stuck. Teflon Obama was no joke. A 52-48 percentage win is respectable.

Sandy is representative of that group of Americans who finally decided "Anybody but the Republicans" and the group that feels it doesn't matter who was wrong or right, the man looks good in that bathing suit.

Media has done its job in America. American's are experts at evaluating media phenomenon. They are inundated with media pitches every day; they sift through all of it with the deftness of seasoned hands. Obama was a star, that was almost enough by itself. Well, it was enough to elect him President of the United States. Of course there is more to the man than rock star attractiveness, but for many who voted for him, it was enough.

As George Patton is reported to have said: "America loves a winner." Obama looked like a winner and he got votes because of it.

Ida Read Obama's Lips:

" It was his face on the TV every night." To Ida, Obama was hope and she liked him; but retired, her home paid for, she was not feeling economic pressure the way some did.

She is dyslexic and had learned to read lips. She would sit with the TV sound down and watch Obama' lips when he talked. She said "he has the best lips." Made her feel all warm. "I watched his lips form words--even with the TV on and the sound up; I watch lips from habit and I watched his. I fell in love with his lips. They moved like Braille music".

Retires have a different relationship with Obama its seems. If they are well off, or making it on social security, or the dead husband's pension, they have more relaxed attitude toward him. Some are wary of him and a significant percentage of this group did not vote for him.

They did not necessarily trust him either. The Chicago stories, Rev. Wright and his so-called "terrorists" friends resonated with many of them—especially when Sarah Palin promoted that image of Obama and his campaign-"Obama may be a nice man but the American electorate should be aware that his friends would gain positions of power and influence in the new administration."

Hillary Clinton alluded to some of these themes as well. For that long summer of 2008 the Clinton campaign found its voice and Obama lost state after state. While the statistics were in his favor and his nomination was inevitable, Clinton none the less made inroads, created doubt and had successes against him.

He won the delegate count, but bloodied and tarnished just a bit. This group gave him the fewest votes.

But the nomination issue settled they appeared to have softened their stances against him in the general election. They supported him in to a greater degree.

Perhaps, they looked at McCain, and as one woman friend said to me: "That man is old. I am old. I know old when I see it." So perhaps the old looked at McCain and went for young.

Obama Summer Photos, Grandma and the Shoebox-Tina's Story;

Virgin Ground

I was the city girl banished to the countryside-to the
grandparents, to learn hard work on the dairy-farm.
The rumbling train after the long flight jumbled my brain;
everything outside that train window bumped along; seemed
jobble-wacky, isolated, and alien; and I felt alone.
I sat next to an older woman who, without looking, whispered
"see the pretty cow?" Her grandchild came from the
bathroom late--a case of identity mistaken.
A pickup truck ride later we were there; passing an old barn,
but finally stopping at a beautiful house.
Grandpa was sitting beside me smelling earthy--gasoline and
fresh dirt--spelling out to me all the summer chores and those
which would be mine.
But, he would help, and show me how to milk the cows.
Grandma's living room was a doily museum, white starched
flower blooms under lamps--some with coasters inside, one
with a flower vase.

This was grandpas and grandmas.

My room was all gingham and florals, muted pinks, greens and
reds- the one Susie had; all her things still preserved there; and
I ran my finger across some of them imagining when she
touched them last; waiting for grandma to close the door.

There was a 4-H photo of Susie and a dairy cow; a
cheerleader's
outfit in the closet; a boy and her with prom roses at the front

door and out of place was a photo of Barack Obama
undoubtedly placed there by Susie herself on a visit home.

Stunned, I hung my clothes in the closet slowly because some
of hers were still there, and, I dropped my tennis bracelet on
the closet floor bent over to pick it up to discover a loose board
there.

I pried at it to see a shoe box barely visible in the dark.
I froze listening close to see if anyone would be coming up;
took my nail file and finished the excavation work;
holding at last in my hand something whose contents I had
already imagined in my mind. What was in Susie's treasure
box, forgotten there?

Easy open; letters wrapped with red ribbon; jewelry; a photo
and other things yet unidentified.

I read around the ribbon to see some letters had stamps and
had been mailed others had not- written but un-mailed. I
opened one
and began to read.

"You are my Virgin Spring; my Thomas flower blooming;
and I am your Virgin Ground".

Struck, should I read on or close the letter and put back the
shoe box top?

There was the Obama's photo staring at me from the dresser now all this linking with the shoebox, the farm, the future and the past.

I put the shoebox back, letter unopened and unread, letting the past be the past and the future have a chance to survive.

Cowboy Gone-The Mother Rejoices:

The mother said she was glad George Bush was gone since the cowboy tough guy image made it bad for little boys who were more intellectual and not fighters. Obama was more like her son and that made her more hopeful for his future.

She recounted the story of her son coming home, tearful having been in his first fight at school. It was more a skirmish than a fight but it was disturbing to him and to her.

What do you say to an eight year old who had a fight with an older black child. Her son had casually said that Obama would not be a bully and would not beat up on younger kids.

After school the older youth waited for him, cornered him. "So you think Obama wouldn't beat your ass? Well I am going to beat your ass. Go tell Obama that."

This little drama is repeated every day in school, irrespective of the race aspect. Schools do not control bullies and the consequences can be devastating for the bullied kids and the school and the parents.

There does not seem to be protection. This major weakness in American social development. It happens to kids in high schools all across the country, irrespective of the neighborhood, color or class. Kids are intimidated and bullied and largely nothing is done about it. School budgets have been slashed and the school personnel feel ham-strung; and have stepped up their efforts to put a stop to this newly discovered problem.

She told her child that he was right. Obama would not be a bully, that he, her child, did what Obama would have done. This was an enormous change to her from George Bush. Cowboy Bush was projected the view fight back and get even. To her bookish, shy child that was not possible. But now with Obama she had an alternate example to give to her boy; and that was important to her boy, perhaps to a generation.
Her note to me was to the point. "Obama is a better example for young boys in my neighborhood."

Obama No. No Way:

Of course, there were many who wrote to say that they would not vote for Obama under any circumstances. Tax and spend liberals, Pastor Wright, Chicago corruption, policies they disagreed with--a number of other reasons surfaced.
Here is one, however, which was striking to me.

No, I Never Would Vote For a Black Man:
This lady in North Carolina could not see herself voting for a black man. It would be going against everything her family and the South stood for she said. Her granddaddy would cry deep in the grave. She knew it was irrational, but, she stated clearly she could not do it. It was point of honor. The South, she noted, was a conquered nation and the true rebels.

She explained it to me in terms or gardening. She was a gardener and she said after years some plants get to be seen as weeds. That is how she felt black people in the United States had come to be seen. Obama's election alone was not going to be enough to change that.

Personally, she treated everyone with respect and was not rude to any one no matter what their color but the United States was a white man's country, built with white man brains and know how, and that was a fact.

Obama would change all that, not him, but the people behind him, people like pastor Wright whom she thought hated white people, hated America and had said as much. People have to stand up to government and not get pushed around. Men have to act like men and not let the government run'em off their land, tax them, take away their property and give it to the blacks, the Mexicans and whatever.

It all wasn't fair in her view and that was what the civil war was all about, Northerners come South to take away what rightful belonged to the South. Slavery was not illegal and slaves were property. You can't take away a man's property without compensation, fairness and due process. That is what happened in the Civil War she said, plain and simple.

Obama as a specter, as someone who threatened property rights and whites specifically, lay there close to the surface during the election and Hillary Clinton's late surge in the Appalachian states makes this evident. But, with the wisdom of hind sight, it is also clear that while there was opposition, it was not deep-seated. New demographic trends were changing the South; changing Appalachian too.

But my North Carolina lady makes some important points. Was the Civil war a regional war over property rights, an economic war of internal imperialism, where the prosperous, industrial North conquered, and impoverished the slave-holding South and gained financially from the war while the

South was laid to waste? Take out the slavery issue and what she asks what was the war really about?
Of course one—you can't take the slavery issue out; two the benefits of Southern life impoverished not only the blacks but the poor whites as well, who died defending a system was benefited only a wealthy few.

History, of course, can be interpreted and reinterpreted, but a pertinent question always is, who in any period, were winners and who were losers and why?

And, this brings us to the small towns of America. How were they reacting to the Obama juggernaut? Are they the modern day losers in the American story?

Small Town America and Obama:

Small towns are suffering. The numbers tell the tale but the numbers don't reveal the human stories behind the statistics. Here is what I have gleaned from a few individuals which I have compiled into a several stories.

Hard Scrabble

Let's call it Hard Scrabble Town outside Scranton, Pa.

"Hillary came, Obama came, but, they didn't bring any jobs with them. I saw him," she said, "took his picture; meantime Hal, my husband couldn't come. He was two towns over looking for work. Further and further he went, further and further he went looking for jobs we both knew were not there, and, would not return no matter what the politicians said."

Her story:
"I was at home one night and Hal didn't come back from looking. I put the kids to bed early and started to watch TV thinking I would hear from him. I called him on the cell but no answer. I called my mom and just casual asked if he was there hoping she would volunteer a little information. I did not want to let on that I was looking for him; didn't want the talk. I also called the bar and pretended I had left my credit card from a week ago asking if Hal was there and if so could he bring it home. But he wasn't there either.

"All year it's been bad," she wrote me. Her husband had been out of work almost two years, taking odd jobs--some an hour or two away-- piling up the driving miles and the time away from home for just enough money to get by and sometimes not

102

enough to get by. Her mother was really good with picking up the kids while she did waitressing at the diner.

Kathy sounded just like Biden's family sitting at the kitchen table counting pennies, trying to get by. And she was apparently very good at it, keeping the family together on a combined income in 2007-2008 of only thirty five thousand dollars a year.

She was aware that some of the women did laundry; some of the women did the men to get extra. She would never do either. And they would not do grass or a meth lab either.

She and Hal would make it on their own—or move if they had to. They had discussed it. If there were no jobs, move to where the jobs were. But, where were the jobs? If they did move, the other places might be more expensive to live; had to pay moving costs, who wants to pay for childcare, when her mother made it easier and she fed the kids too?

That night she turned the TV off and went outside to start the car. Where was he? Many things started to run through her mind. Was he unhappy; was he off with some other woman? Had he left her?

She ran the last few months back in her mind. Was there something that she could point to that might mean he was gone; that he was unhappy?

There had been little time for sex. She thought about that. She thought about his face the times she said she was tired. And she was tired. The boys took all her energy and she wasn't getting any younger.

The bar flies can make a man feel special and any man can fall. Any man can have his thing fall right out of his pants, if the moment is right.

She went out to take a smoke in the car--she never smoked in the house and lit up. She wasn't supposed to. Hal would be upset if he knew she still smoked once in a while, but she felt she needed a smoke right now, and took a deep drag. and dialed his cell phone for fifth time that evening.
Night time, night time you could hear the cricket chirping away.

He had to know she would be worrying. Why wouldn't he call her? It must be something real bad.

She ran through her mind far-fetched ideas-since she had exhausted the logical ones. Was he is some ditch dead and dying? She thought she should go look but where would she look and she didn't want to leave the boys alone. He could be in some hospital unconscious. He could be dead.

His father was an hour away and feeling poorly. He could have gone to see him.

Exhausted, she got out the car, put the cigarette out, and when to check on the boys. They were fine. Sinking onto the couch, she lay back and fell asleep, awakening with a start at the sound of the car.

He was back. The engine quit but he did not get out right away. He was apparently just sitting in the damn car. She waited; finally the car door opened. It was him, she knew his footsteps. She waited in the dark with the TV sound down. She waited not knowing what to do.

The clock said 2am. The door latch clicked and he stood there, not seeing at first in the shadows, but noticing the TV light. He came over putting out his hand to turn the TV off and then noticed her.

"Katie, damn it you scared me", he said jumping. "What are you doing up?"

"Waiting on you. You didn't call. I was worried. Where were you?"

"Sorry," he said, "I should have. I got a chance to do 4 to midnight at the plant in Buford, so I stepped in for a guy whose wife was in the hospital. Nothing permanent but got the 10 hours."

She stirred on the couch and reached out to him and gave him her hand. He took it. She noticed the pained look in his eye.

She said. "I'm just glad you are alright."

"Did you hear? Obama won."

"I heard" Hal said. "Maybe he can do something."

This story is a compilation but undoubtedly one which was and is being repeated all over the country.

Hard Scrabble Bubble Gum-Small Town Blues:

But who are small town people who remain in the small towns, who don't leave who didn't leave as young adults. Who stick it out on main street? Who are they? And, what effect if any, did Obama have on them?

Well, from my correspondences they include the small farmers who still eeking out a living, the professionals--doctors and lawyers whose practices serve sometimes several communities on a rotating basis, people who live off the truckers coming through, tourists if there are any and those like this lady, I met her on a trip going north in California. I stopped along the way to use the John. She accosted me saying,

"You going up to the casinos are ya" (I wasn't.)

Her face was hard and it had marks on it and she was smoking her cigarette when I walked in to use the John.

 I nodded to her saying "have to use the john."

'You probably rich, buy me a drink why don't ya? '
I said 'sure, when I come back'

I came back to stand up cowboy style along side her at the bar and she started talking to me like I was her best friend.

'These women in here don't appreciate a gentleman like your self and they sure as hell don't buy drinks for a lady."

Her voice was hard as below-the-seat bubble-gum with a hard scrabble tone above a hacking cough.

"I was married once but he couldn't handle the ride; needed me a real man and he got all upset-started to hit me. It was plain to see he wasn't right in the head; wanted all the time to be lovey-dovey after."

"Hell a man, I always say, has to be 6 feet tall to take a ride on me.
He wasn't and ran off with the carnival that come through town."

"How about another one? Mattie, come on over here the gentleman is buying drinks."

Mattie smiled a single tooth...

"Thanks" she said.

She kept the conversation going.
"People look at me and they think what happened to her? Life is what happened to me. Life is what happened to me. Made bad decisions--never got out of this town--stayed too long and now I ain't fit to live no where else 'ceptin' here. A misfit living among all the other misfits around here. We all misfittin' together."

"Gotta go." I said. "One more?" she said.

I drove away thinking how much of life is random luck--good and bad choices--and circumstance.

Small town people sometimes have a strong sense that they are small towners and some feel stuck in that small town atmosphere.

They have adapted to it, feel more comfortable in it. They, some, can't really see them selves successfully competing in the city. In the small town they have a place, perhaps some standing as well. They can manage expenses and can't afford city prices in any event.

Soon, after not leaving, it feels like at some point it is too late to leave. They are rooted, can't leave even if they wanted to. "Mis-fittin" as it was expressed to me.

These are part of the "guns and religion" group Obama's comment referred to. He knew them. They are heart-landers.

He spoke, not as an outsider, but as a Been-To; been to college, been to the city etc. Been To is an expression which was described to me by one of the "Never-Lefts."

This group has only one question, "what can you do for me and my small town." The question at this writing remains unanswered.

Women, Small Towns and The Covent

If small town older women have reconciled themselves to small town life, younger women in these small towns have not. With the recession, they have seen their changes of marriage, even in a small town severely diminished. Young men are unemployed, gone away or idle. These younger women feel that the promise of America, the house, the car, the children and the security are not in their future.

They have taken things into their own hands. They have discovered the internet. They are searching for Mr. Right in unprecedented numbers, mostly through online dating sites which have exploded in terms of their membership. Since women, at the same time are going to college in greater numbers than the men they are now expressing deep disappointment in life, in men and in their future prospects.

Who is Mr. Right today for this group? It used to be Mr. Steady Job. Today women are looking for studs, they are following a Paris Hilton pattern of undressing on internet dating sites to compete with young girls from other small towns who are literally advertising their bodies also on the new sites.

The new sites are catering to this group of small town party girls, the prettiest girls in town who think with a racy photo the might get discovered, find a rich husband, have a reason to relocate and change their lives. The old letters the love-lorn, the e-harmony type sites have been overwhelmed by the sex and party sites and the anti has been upped by exponential degrees. The men are the women these women have divorced looking for party girls with no strings attached, or the un-marrieds who are jobless.

Both are being manipulated by some of the newer sites with names like lust, horny, sex search scream their real purpose—make money off young girls from small towns who now are willing to take in all off thinking they will find Mr. Right, or

Mr. Sugar Daddy, or Mr. Party, or Mr. Hung.
Bad times always results in the phenomenon where women seek other alternatives when they realize that male partners are scare or non-existent. It is an extension of the Women's Movement which was not anticipated. Many of these sites are owned by a few porn-financed conglomerates and make millions, are unregulated and offer scams, take personal information and sell it to spammers, often are fronts for prostitution as well.

Down-sized America, less affluent America means the young have to do things they won't ordinarily do to survive. Since they saw Paris Hilton do sex tapes and survive, in their young lives this seems normal.

Small Town Malaise: "Just the Red Meat Please--Hold the Malaise."

Jimmy Carter's Malaise is alive and well in small towns in America. No jobs, no prospects, no land, no money, bad times. Old identities and roles die, and, new ones not yet born. This is an English teacher in a junior college.

All Metaphor and Malaise Now

Our town has become a metaphor;
We live only shadows of our old lives, not what we used to be and yet not anything new or even satisfying. We are dying the slow death of a town that the highway passed by.
The men drink at the bar, the women complain.
The men drink at the taverns that are still located just outside shut factory doors.
You look at them and they look like they half expect the factory doors will open again and they will pick up the lunch pails and go to work as usual.
I do ok at the college, she told me but, my husband has had a hard time finding work, most of it is temporary; he works and then he is out of work.
There is a bad taste to life now.
He watches the TV, to the weather channel. The weather channel for hours at a time.
We all can't remember who we are; who we were.
What's happed to this country is a damned shame,
and they have stripped us of the ability to fight back.
No, work, no dignity.
The government, the politicians, the wall street greedy people

have sold out the middle class in this country.
I said to myself give the black guy a chance.
Might work and can't get worse.

John--The Hunting is Bad:

He had an injury and had to give up hunting. He hated Obama's comment about God and guns and his wife said he sat sunk deep into his lounging chair. She said that not being able to hunt was killing him, he loved it so. Her marriage felt dead to her.

My view of her sentiments:

<u>Hunting</u>

"Where" she said, one day "does your love live?
Is it in your eyes? I have looked there; I look there every day.
Is it in your heart?
I know it beats but some days it is so faint;
in your mind?
Tell me where your love for me gone? "

He said,
"I was taught that deeds and providing is where my love shows;
in being sure everyone here is safe and that there is enough for what everyone needs or wants. I am not good at flowery words or affection even. I wish I were better. For you."

"What about you? Where does your love for me live?" She said,
"It is everywhere with me--in my heart, it pounds you know

still for you--In the house. I place my love in flower vases, In the vacuum cleaner; in the dinners I make; in the wine served. In my thoughts and emotions. I remember everything we've ever done."

He said: "I wish I had that ability you have. I think I am made for the hunt.

"But now," he said "there is no hunt."

Make no mistake elections are not just about policy. White men in America, especially older white men did not like their wives and neighbors fawning over the black candidate. They also knew that many of them, the women especially, were doing it to irritate them.

But the underlying dilemma of the men, not just while males are that there traditional roles in the family, as providers were under attack and had been for many years.

Real wages in America have not gone up since 1968- when a single wage-earner could support the family. The wife could stay home with the kids.

Today males have seen their wives forced out of the home into the work-place. Where one wage-earner was enough to support a family in 1968 that is clearly not the case in 2009- and getting worse. Women once in the work-place moved toward independence, threatening further traditional male roles in the family.

But in the mid-west and for the human race apparently, the hunt which had been the male contribution to the family is over. (Mailer has suggested this is the secret attraction of war for southern American males. War is a re-institution of the hunt.)

If the hunt is over what is to be the role of the male? In small towns it is the specter too of the failure to make the farm work, or having to farm and take a part-time job as well; it is having to become a wage-slave in the new factory, or the minimum wage clerking job at the new Wal-mart. It is seeing your kids having to leave your town, and losing their support in keeping the family farm or business going—another blow. It might be seeing your wife having to teach, or take in laundry, or wait tables as the local diner.

All this does not sit well with the American male of lore. Religion is embraced as supportive of traditional male roles and support in bad times. It is not just God it is neighbors to help with loans, repairs and money when needed; it is networking. The guns harked to the hunt; male bonding around the hunt and guns and, for some a reaction against minorities, Mexicans, liberals, Wall Street is all understandable.

And here comes Obama.

Well, he is not perfect, and he is black but the anger against Wall Street, the Republicans, the Media, whoever is not stronger than the need to fix the dinner-table issues.

Are you going to vote your ideology or your wallet? This was the issues in diners, at the kitchen tables, at family gatherings:

Wallet or ideology; Republican assurances of the status quo or Obama's promise to put food on the table.

The wallet attraction was strong enough to have many while males give Obama a chance. They held their noses, checked their checkbooks and went for the hope of a financial turn-around with the bright black guy from Chicago.

Moving Inward: Small Town Defense:

The reaction to hard times makes many males go inward; becoming more non-communicative, self blaming, and distant from their wives, children and families. Here as some samples of that reaction.

Tom and his wife discussed this openly, He told her he felt that he was failing them as a family and didn't know what to do. He felt ashamed and embarrassed as well. He had stopped talking because he had nothing to say; that it was not a talking problem, that talking about getting a job for the one lost was not going to help.

She said that she felt anxious and lonely when he clammed up like that and the kids too. They felt him distance himself from them.

They needed him to talk, to be there for them.
But Tom said he couldn't. It was all he could do to have that talk with her that night. He just couldn't talk about it everyday. That would be too much.

This inwardness is another aspect of bad economic times. Tom apparently began to spend more and more time with his buddies who were in similar straits. Not working, few prospects, living only with the support of unemployment and help from his wifes family and a little from his own-- it didn't help that the family savings were torn apart.

All they really had was the house left them by his wife's mother. It was paid for but needed repairs and there was little money for that; and, paid for or not the taxes had to be paid.

At last check-in, they still don't talk, although she noted he seemed interested in retraining in some green industry ideas Obama talked about- roofing and household insulations which save energy. But nothing concrete is currently available.

The Toll on Small Town Families:

Wisconsin Mother age 35:

"I never knew my Dad, not really. He was always working, and, when home he plopped down in front of the TV set. The Obama's seem so happy and he is always talking about Michelle and the girls. It was great to see the grandmother move into the White House too. They all eat breakfast together."

This letter and several others express this situation. This sentinel dad syndrome. Dad spends his time working, sometimes two jobs; sometimes he does lots of overtime. Summer time he is a fire-fighter and makes as much as possible; and winters he works in a local auto repair shop. But there is a quiet depression in the household. The mom feels that he ignores the daughter.

He apparently feels that making a living is his job and raising the children is her job. Out of that comes a sense, in this female, that her dad didn't really spend time with her; and bought presents when what she wanted was his time, his attention or a hug.

As, the daughter grew older, she came to understand someone must play the sentinel role while others "sit the warming fire." My rendering the emotional content of this situation: "Love seen and unseen; Father-soldiers are born, and, then they die.

His duty stoked on rampart high; his wick burned low each
night; occasionally I'd see ember sentiments float by; muted,
inarticulate; love's firefly's extent just beyond my child's eye.
So cruel this:
Security and Love bent by circumstance—both he and I."

How I Voted and Why--Charlotte

I got married in June, 2008 when Obama looked to be having trouble with the election. My dad is voted for McCain in the primary, and will too, in the election. I will vote Obama because I want to. My finance, too.
But the wedding, which cost my Dad a lot of money, was a little tense. I wrote up her story below in lyrical prose.

Summer Wedding Autumn Dad

I was a summer blossom given away; walking before a tear-scented wedding train, inside an arm-locked processional, with attending musical strains, and rose-petal aisled marriage vows.

My Dad finally breathed-not wanting to release but, willed himself.
Love leaves that autumn-mixing then separations and matrimonies,
ironies and cleavings, all falling gently from his tree; floating evolving-winging paradoxes and meanings- leaf rustlings stirring;
signaling someone's winter and someone's spring.

Dad cries.

Daughter loves both autumn leaves and summer blossomings; a gardenia scent falls quietly in the heavy air, memory stroked; trembling new times; an election year.
He and I still can't talk politics.

In Bad Times Love Is The Only Safe Harbor:

Americans, among these respondents often rely upon renewing their love for one another as a shield against turbulent times. Incredible sentiments flow from this. Here is one I have put to lyrical prose expressed to me by a lady who revealed that she and her husband had renewed their vows election week.

Velvet Harbor

Lay me down won't you? Open my Book of Hearts; read every page tonight; touch my shinning face for it always gleams in our candle light.
Breathe onto my closed eyes the gentle wind that loves me.

Hold my hand in this night transferring that love hands do; lay my skirt aside flower-petal style my blouse is milky, cloud white and I see me reflected in your dark eyes.
My universe begins to rise and I am lost inside you.
Suspend us on bedroom air softly fluttering in time where we sail those loving seas and land in the dark velvet harbor where we renew our vows the You and I husband and wife:
We will beat all the odds--Love is our shielding.

Examining the Past, Reconciling to the Future:

The campaign for some was an exercise in examining what they wanted from government, many shifting allegiances from Republican voting patterns over to Obama and the democrats.

These were not easy decisions from many to make. This shift had gotten started in 2004, accelerated in the voting patterns in 2006. By 2008 Obama was the beneficiary of those shifts as well as having accelerated them.
This period was one where individuals examined their relationships, and their lives. It was clear that the campaign of 2008 was to be an historic one for many reasons. And it was.

This lady mentioned that Obama seemed to be a nice man and genuinely charming. That charm reminded her of her husband of 27 years and their courtship. I was charmed by the story because it has all of the values mid-westerners really like. Resourcefulness, determination, and confidence—things that, for many, Obama exhibited. See what you think.

He approached her at the hardware story she worked and said that he had seen her picture on the cover of one of the novels on the shelf in the back. (a romance novel, it turns out.)

He said with a sly simile she looked prettier in person. So began his courtship of her.

He came back two days later told her that she was the women he was going to marry. She told him, thanks but pigs would fly before she married a local and got stuck "in this town forever."

He smiled his dazzling smile and left.
The next day he arrived in pick-up truck with a pig in the flat-bed, unloaded the pig and strapped wings on the pig; parading the pig up and down the sidewalk in front of the store yelling

"Pig to fly on runway nine. Pig to fly on run-way niner"
It was cute but she was still not convinced, he was the one for her.

He showed up days later wearing a gingham dress over his blue jeans, standing at the counter, turning and turning, modeling the dress for her saying he was saving up to buy it for her since she told him she liked gingham dresses.
The ridiculousness of it was, well charming.

She agreed to see him but first he would have to come to the house and meet her parents. That night he showed up with a box of cigars for her mother and a box of used golf balls for her dad. Both looked at him but soon that wonderful charm of his kicked in and they both decided they liked him.

She got into his car noticing that the trunk had no lid; noticing that on the passenger side of the car there was a hole and you could see the road.

She drove away listening to him talk about his dreams and plans for their eventual marriage; saying that there was no hurry; that he was willing to be as patient as he needed to be, to give her time to be sure that the "casserole was ready done" before she took it out of the oven."

They did marry and while pigs didn't fly one tired and that turned out to be good enough.

Also, she had read that when Michelle met Obama, on one of their first dates, he drove a car with a hole on passenger side too.
She thought that was somehow a sign. Her now, husband, thinks so too.

Grandmother Magic:

If hard times causes all to step up and make suggestions or review their memories, relationships and circumstances, here is one from a grandson about a family tradition—about what his family did to cope with bad times. It had been passed down for generations in his family. I include it to illustrate the point that when reality fails people often begin to rely upon acts of faith.

Mark's Story of the Grandmothers:

Each of us when we reached 14, would make the visit to Grandmothers' house to see what was inside her Treasure Box; the Family Treasure Box where each year one of us got to see what she had hidden there.
My Dad had been, my older brother had been, and now it was my turn to see that part of Family History.

No one who'd seen could talk of it. No one could reveal to anyone what was in Grandma's secret box.
No one did. No one would risk Grandmother's upset.

She lived beneath the 'L' in Chicago refusing to move and they built the tracks right over her house; each time one passed it rocked her house like rolling thunder; varoom, clacky clack--another one going by. Stubborn was not the word for Grandmother. She still wrote letters 30 years later to every Mayor complaining about the tracks and the trains saying she wanted them torn down.

Every month a letter. Grandmother never gave up; never forgot; fierce in her loves, fierce about her neighborhood, fierce about things which displeasured her, fierce about family, fierce about everything.

I sat with her, apron on: she served me pie. 'Sonny' she said now you at the age where you need to learn grown-up things. Like your Dad and brother your turn now come to see what drives this family; our family heirloom so to speak. You'll see now.

As you grow up you hear people talking about it but we are the only family that has it in our treasure box. Lot's want it but we the only one are that has it.

She walked me up her tiny narrow stair case to the attic my head spinning, wondering what it could be.

What did we have in our family that the whole world wanted? The treasure box was small; a faded gold color with a hand-carved lid covered by Grandma's liver-spotted hand which shook in the dim light.

She shifted the box opening it with a tiny key smiling faintly, her eyes moistening as a sliver of sunlight reflected into the opening box; and, I could just begin to see what was inside. 'There it is' she said 'What is it? 'I said, staring at a piece of cloth; satin sheen with a lace border. "Every since your great grandmother got it, it has been the luck of this family and so people's all over the world hear about it but we the only one's who got it. 'What is it?"

"Your great great grandmother's; cut from her mother's wedding dress and from that day this families' luck changed."

I looked at her eyes looking for an answer there. "Grandma what is it?"

"You heard of the Silver Lining?"

"Yes." I said.

"Well this family has the only one. It is the Silver Lining from your great, great, grandmothers wedding dress."
Grandma had it and she believed it had saved our family all these years.

"I took it out when your mother had her cancer and she got better and it took away her pain. I took it out when your younger brother had his accident, and he lived. I took it out when your grandfather went to war and he came home safe. I take it out when ever this family needs things. It is our Silver Lining.

Now you must never speak or tell what is in the treasure box or it will break the spell."

I never did to this day and now you know.

He Had Aura: What is the Obama Magic?

"I believe in angels and I swore from the first day he had one on his shoulder. That man had aura. Someone, or something, was moving obstacles out his way, cleared his path, and elevated him to be our President.

You have to believe in divine intervention. Many, many angels, I believe, landed on American shoulders on election day and whispered to millions, if not billions, "Give Obama a Chance to be President And we did."

(Carol wrote me from Omaha)

One report I understand states that 80% of Americans believe in angels that intervene and take an active part in our lives. Whether true or false it was clear to many that Obama seemed to have divine support in his entire career, not just the run for the Presidency.

He won a senate seat by taking advantage of the voter registration laws. He won a US senate seat when the opposition self-destructed in a sex-scandal and he won in a landslide. He endured any number of potential set-backs in her campaign, Wright, Ayers, radical charges, charges of homosexuality, and attacks from both the right and the left. The Clinton campaign seriously under-estimated him did not see soon enough the importance of the caucus system. This perfectly matched Obama's campaigns style his organizing skills his temperament and background.

Indeed it does, for some, look like angels were watching over Obama. And they said so.
I came across this assertion many times. People lit candles for before Iowa and believed it made a difference, People lit candles for him after New Hampshire and believe it made a difference.

Moral of this story. Don't underestimate the power of the angels.

Teen-Town Is Holed Up in the Bedroom Suffering From High School:

There are, perhaps, millions teen-agers holed up in their bed-rooms all across this country, feeling left out, alienated, angry, suicidal and hopelessness and misunderstood; many on the verge of giving up on life.

Obama has meant to a lot of them. Not all, but to many. But, the teen-world is a hard one and even Obama only penetrated marginally for what I could discern.

See the sentiments in this next selection from Michelle.

They Don't Like Me

"They don't like me
and it won't change; ever.
Not just them, but, others too.
I try.
I try.
I talk to them;
try to be nice
but they don't like me
and they will sometimes
pretend
to like me
but they don't.
They don't really like me
even when they try
and I don't like them
because they don't like me--

131

and not liking me --proves they are bad people;
even though I don't like them either
but, that is different
because they didn't like me first."

The high school world can be a rock-hard world as every
parent of high school children know.

Teens and Obama" Upheaval and Historical Change May Not Be Noticed:

Whatever, the foment in the political arena, many teens remained outside the excitement of it all, preoccupied with personal issues. I came to see that the high school experience as harmful to too many teens and, as adults later in life, many regarded the high school years as the most damaging period in their lives.

No matter what age, most American's still smart from those middle school hurts and harms.

Cory is an example where he felt his sanity had been harmed. Cory had a rough time of it high school. Small in stature, bookish and acne-scared, he felt high school ruined his life. He dropped out; started to do drugs, went into the army but was dishonorably discharged for reasons I am not clear about. He was on powerful drugs for mental health issues; back and home living with his parents. I have just pieces of his story. Who Am I? -Cory's Story

I am running all the time I'm running down hill; I am thinking all the time but clear thinking is foggy to me most times. I do things sometimes and can't remember what. I do things sometimes and can't remember why.

I have days I just want not to see no one; just want to hide. I think certain days others are looking at me. I think certain days others are better than me. I don't want to go into certain things in detail-the detail will hurt, need to keep it general and light, not get too heavy in my mind.

Don't want to be like others because I can't. Don't want to adjust because it will make me crazy. I prefer people think I am dull and lazy rather than I've tried and failed.

Don't want any one to get to know me too well; I might be judged.

I have a secret side of me know one knows that is superior over others.

I run away from feeling down and tried being happy; the drugs made me feel happy but didn't like it; it didn't work out too well.

What is wrong with me? I was born in the wrong century I should be a pirate and not polite or effete.

And another thing I really like being around people but I don't really like them to talk to me. And another thing; I really didn't like high school."

Cory is voter-eligible. He didn't really respond to my questions on Obama. He didn't really pay much attention to politics. His personal concerns were over-whelming him.

But he and other teens are the next troops in the Obama army as he seeks re-election. Many, 14 or 15 now will be able to vote next time around.

This point is not lost on the Obama strategists. The stakes are high because this group is influenced heavily by the opinions and voting patterns of their older brothers and sisters and by young adults they come into contact with.

If they go Obama, they will tend to vote the same way the rest of their lives. If the go Obama, and many will, the democrats could have a generational advantage for many years to come.

These teens matter. And the ones I came into contact with on the internet tended to be the troubled ones; and what troubles they have indeed.

They often, feel unsure of themselves. Not unusual, but more pronounced in some teens that others. I heard from teens that cut themselves regularly, of course, drugs, or have had sex experiences that left them bitter and angry. Many of the young female teens are angry, bitter about their experiences with young males.

There are the abused teens, one's living with drug-taking parents, meth-lab households--selling grass--anything the parents can do to make a living in a small town.

Many have locked themselves in their bedrooms, walled themselves off from parents, interacting mostly on the internet, watching cartoons and TV shows; vampire shows, reality shows; all of which gives them a decidedly false sense of the world outside their small towns.

They hunger for a message that they will ok, despite their current circumstances, To some extent Obama's message of hope has reached some of them but with little effect. They are the hostage generation, hostage to the times, fewer and fewer prospects for a future and parents who seem less and less able to help. These are the limbo generation kids 12-16 who seem to be suffering the most. Young adults, have some college and some foothold on the adult world. These youngsters have none of that confidence-building experience. They are suffering.

Another example:

Mary's Right to Exist:

Mary (14) makes a powerful argument that some of us don't exist to some others of us. Whether it be invisible blacks, the invisible ugly people, the invisible foreigners; women sometimes feel invisible. Invisibility is real. Many youngsters as well as adults who smart under it—are angry because of it. My summary of Mary's story below.

I Want to Exist- Mary's Story

Answer me this; riddle me that; enigma-surrounded I retreat, to the isolated and the cruel snide for solace--against you and others who think this is a debate, or argument,--when for me it is about whether I exist.
No, gentlemen, ladies we engage here not in idle gossip wars-- for me this is more serious-- and masks, (despite my telling my self it is less than that,) the fact that for me mental survival is at stake here; all the more so when I see it is not that way for you; it makes me feel smaller still that you can play with life-- indeed, even in this conversation; as if for you nothing is a stake; oblivious to, that for me, all is at risk-- the half-healed wound stabbed again.

There is no quarter here asked for or given here; you must die in this conversation for me to have just one moment to exist; as I resist, illogically, to save myself.

All this I know sounds crazy; through all this I am aware that none of it makes sense; But, if I had control I would resist.

The point is I don't--and I can't--and I must save not only myself but all the others too who are invisible-- to avoid the mental obituary that life seeks to write for me and them every day, each day, in every situation.
They are playing for the joy of the game; I am playing for the right to exist.
Crazy? I know. I don't know what is wrong with them. Why can't they see what they are doing to me? Why are they so out of touch with reality?

Tell me who is the crazy one? Why is my reality the crazy one?

This rule makes no sense. It is well, crazy, to deny me what I need to exist- which is after all the need to maintain my dignity in the face of the brutal facts of my life; I really don't matter; no special talents; one among a mass average- when everyone says I am special in some way but, in fact I know I am not- I am average, barely having a rationale to exist.

There it is. So does this all mean I have no value?
No, I exist. There is the problem: people treat me at though I don't."

There is not much to be added to this powerful statement.

After the Teen Years You Have to Grow Up For Real:

Love Anita: Young People Struggle To Grow Up:

The Anita Journal has been around on the internet for several years. The entries are apt now as they were in terms of touching upon how difficult it is for young people to find direction in life and make the transition to adult hood.

Obama had, and continues to have, a profound impact upon the 18-35 groups. I hear from them, read their Blogs, poems and essays from small towns all over America. I have excluded horrific materials on rape, self-cutting, rage, beatings, Goths, drugs and violence, meth labs and cannabis, the omnipresent high school hatreds, and, of course sex. But, understand, it is there. The younger demographic will determine the shape of American politics, if Obama is the prototype, for years. This next piece asks the question how is it going to be possible to grow up in the Obama age now in this age of uncertainty?

Right now young people feel it the most and have the most to lose.

Below Anita writes in her journal. I have altered a few things but retain the substance of the entry.

After All This-Happiness

There is a drunk boy in my bed and he smells.
I want him to leave so I can wash the sheets,
clean up, arrange things and erase this episode
in my single hood.

Scandal, scandal, scandal, boy's boy's boys:
woke up this morning, no love in the bed.

You and I should meet for lunch. You can give me
advice. I sometimes feel judged. But, that is from my
friends who aren't getting any.

Right now I guess I am wrapped up in the excitedness of it all.
But, it is getting lonely here because most of my friends are
getting
married.

One day, after all of this I will be married and happy and all
that.

Love, Anita.

But the simple question remains: where is the future and what
does it hold for the Anita's of the world? Meantime she on
hold, partying, looking for work, or working at unsatisfying
jobs, immersed in friends, TV shows, hot guys, gossip
networks, sexual adventuring, and pushing the future further
and further away because today seems endless and
unchanging, at least in terms of her prospects.

Molly in New York Debutanting and Dating:

This is a rendering of the sentiments of a 21yr old new to the
New York dating scene. Molly looked to a new kind of life
under Obama. Not as articulate as I have re-created here, but,
the underlying thought is all about having the tools to become
a whole person in the process of maturing. Obama is young
enough for young people like Molly to see him as a role-model
of real growth and development into a person she'd like to be
herself.

Gauzy Friends and Youth

Add to me slithered hope
lather on time telescoped:
I aspire to grow
larger than I am.

Piece together small achievements;
test my dreams against cubicle worlds
and gauzy friends
shadow boxing.

I cannot yet define who I am
so I invent pieces of me
to fill in the gaps reality leaves
in between
traces of my apartment life.

How can I mature
in these panoplies
where I never see

experience full scoped?

Fragmented life
in shattered pieces
distends the human mind.

If failures and hopes
are not mine
and only facsimiles of same,

then, my life is not my own,
experience itself interstitial.

Some days,
I suffice
to queue
and wait to be-
imagining that
I am becoming
the am
I'm currently not.
But in all this
I can see
I'll breech the abyss-

dreams my sturdy bridge;
til that day I am whom

I used to dream
I'd be.

The young adult world is now one where few of them have gone into the sciences or math. Our graduate schools are filled with those from other countries. Our young adults are in the business schools and the law schools. Our manufacturing base has been decimated. Unions are weak and don't provide the clout to fund an American middle class life for the non-college educated. These two groups, both middle class by income or education face a bleak future.

Obama is banking on green jobs and infrastructure rebuilds for the older folks and renewal in the education system for the young group plus national service. No one has told this latter group that many will have to re-locate to other countries where the jobs of the future lie. No one has that kind of political courage-yet.

Meantime the young adult gyrate to the cities where they preoccupy themselves with interstitial living styles.

Here is Beth's story.

Growing Up and Young Adult Hood:

Beth's Bed-Time Story—New York Style

She was new to New York and dating New York style took some getting used to. This Beth's dating story in New York in October of 2008. (This is a summary of her letter to me, put into a story format.)

She met him at an Obama volunteer group. She was new to New York and she thought it would be a good way to meet people. Out of college in the mid-west she was alone in the big apple with admittedly vague plans about get some modeling work, if not, she was interested in being a casting director. A friend of hers was doing that in New York and had invited her along to the volunteer meet-up.

Randy was nice, from the mid-west: Detroit. He smelled of Old Spice and that reminded Beth of home and her granddad. She thought he was cute. She knew from his attention, that he liked her. They had an instant rapport. Randy was a political science major and looking to go to law school after a year of working as a legal intern in a New York law firm. Actually, a pretty impressive job. Hundreds had applied, Randy had gotten the job.

It was easy to see why. He was informed, and had a quiet way of talking and making his points, but leaving odd little spaces in the conversation in which Beth spoke up, often saying things to break the silence, she surprised herself with her own views.

Randy seemed to make her own self-expression easier.
Randy was saying that Obama was going to win and all that
Hillary could do was to create rancor among democrats and
make his mandate smaller than it should be.

He paused and looked at her. Beth did not pay much attention
to politics but Randy was looking her expecting her opinion,
Beth surprised her self by saying yes, but Hillary is also
mobilizing a lot of women for democrats that didn't think
about politics before.

The truth was, she Beth, was an example. Randy nodded, his
silent agreement at Beth's point. Beth felt good she had said it,
good that Randy had recognized it.

That was how the relationship began, and progressed over two
dates, which were fun. They talked a lot.

The third date Beth knew would be different. She would have
to decide whether to let the relationship go on; Randy was
showing signs of wanting to make things more permanent and
showing signs of being interested in her sexually.
She didn't really know how she felt about the sex. Lot's of
issues there.

He picked her up and obviously meant the evening to be
special-he handed her flowers at the door and actually had rose
petals in the cab on the way to dinner. Nice touch.
Well dinner and two bottles of wine they were at this small
studio apartment and they did make love.

He was a shock to her in several ways. First he was very sweet and slow. He didn't rush things; they listened to music for two hours before he made a move. He told her that if it was too soon he would be fine with that. She decided to go ahead and make love with him.

He surprised her in his body. He had a great body that did not show in his clothes and he seemed comfortable inside that body.

He was very smooth, walked smooth, and floated sort of. Beth was not comfortable naked and she used her clothes as a shield getting into bed.

In bed she was surprised at how the love-making really affected her. She lost touch with her usual caution and moved with Randy, they became a couple in bed and she was left shaking, her thighs were shaking and she tried to hide it. She felt light-headed and suddenly feeling that something had happened; that this had affected her in some deep way. She wanted more, to cuddle and he obliged without her even asking. He sensed it had affected her as well.

He went to the bathroom and Beth lay alone thinking through the ramifications of the evening's love making.
She didn't really know Randy, she had no idea about aids, herpes, his family, his friends. She had no idea of what he was going to be expecting. Sex on every date now? She wasn't sure she was into that.

He may leave the intern ship in a year for law school and then where would she be?

Had making love with him been a big mistake; in fact a humiliation in which she had let the wine make her do something she would not have done otherwise?

Suppose he never called her after that night?

She could hear him coming back from the bathroom. She could just leave and see if he called her, see if he was really interested in continuing the relationship and of so why? She could put her cell phone on vibrate and wait for that call and pretend the evening and the sex never happened. If he didn't call how would that feel?

Well, in that moment she decided she would not just leave and wait for a call. Something did happen and she would be lying to herself to deny that it didn't. She would ask him what his intentions were. But, no wait. He would think she was asking for some big commitment and she wasn't. She didn't really know if she wanted to see him again.

To bring it up, to talk about their relationship in the future or not was like pulling on the wings of a butterfly and hoping they don't break.

He came back and sat down and noticed the expressions on her face and asked if she was ok. She lied and said "oh, I'm fine. Thanks for dinner and everything…" She used his technique of speaking and then letting a silence happen, forcing the other person to commit, to speak, to react. She finished waiting for his response.

"Are you sure you are ok?" His response was a question. Her heart pounded. He was avoiding everything.

He must have read her mind. He had moved slowly across the tiny space between them and touched her hand.

"I don't know, I mean I didn't expect... that I would be so ah affected by being with you tonite. But I did want you to know that it was the best evening of my life. No strings though. No pressure. Just wanted you to know. I am thinking that we just see how it goes from here. You don't know me really and you need time, I need time. But I am willing to give us time in this thing. How about you?"

I have gone into detail here because for youth adults casual love-making is a very serious matter; serious because in times of uncertainty whom you marry or hook-up with is a life changing decision; serious because love-making can be a life and death decision; serious because two people are hooking-up who are still in the process of finding out who they are. They are unformed personalities, unformed still in the maturation process. Casual sex is not casual.

Everything is affected by the context of electing a president in crisis times. Everything, including who you decide to have sex with after a date.

But assuming all these gauntlets are managed, what is to be the happy future this future couple can look forward to. Unknown at this point.

Election Night Stories:

There were many election night stories—where were you when you heard the news that Barack Obama had won the election as President of the United States? People will remember it the way an earlier generation remembered where they were on the day they heard the news about Jack Kennedy, Martin Luther King, Bobby Kennedy; these were generational events. The election of Obama is a similar generational event—and lodged in the memory banks of millions, if not billions of people around the globe.

I have included just a few of these election night stories.

A Tale of Two Breasts:

First Sister Hug After the Surgery Is Nonetheless Joyful: (They volunteered for Obama.)

Two sisters Gloria and Brenda were watching the returns election night after Gloria's breast surgery. She had her breast removed three weeks before the election and the two sisters had agreed to watch the returns together.
Their excitement was, of course, high and the tension was palatable. First encouraging signs; Barack wins Florida; Barack wins Pennsylvania, and finally Indiana. And then the realization: Obama has been elected President of the United States.
Brenda's note says that at that point they hugged and she noticed, and sister noticed, that the breast was missing. First time it had hit. Her baby sister had had a breast removed.

Brenda said," don't you worry baby, Barack's going to put that stem cell research back and our young girls will have a chance-- won't have to worry about this breast cancer thing."

The point here is that this election was personal. Obama had called for hope and hope meant that millions of people who took their personal hopes and dreams into the voting booth, voted for Obama expecting that he would see that those dreams became a reality. To arouse that kind of faith is a tremendous achievement and a tremendous responsibility, one that can be elevating and powerfully important to a politician but also very very dangerous if those hopes are dashed.

(I in later chapters ask the question so what is the future of this Obama inspired Hope.)

Election Night Poets:

Hope always brings out the poets. Hope always stokes the dream machine. Election night was an absolutely magical night for millions of Americans and much of the world.

The first decade of the 21st century had not brought good news. the planet seemed in peril, the global financial systems seemed about to teeter and fall, food riots, unemployment, global warming.

It was a night to give Hope a chance to stamp out some of the embers of despair. Obama, that night, his campaign, did have that effect on many. And the poets wanted to write about that moment.

Every poet picked up his or her pen election night and tried to write. History was being made and that moment deserved the poets regard.

Here are a two of my own contributions:

This first poem was written the day before the election and the second one after the election results were known.

America Votes: The Plebiscite of the Soul:

In America
we vote tonite
on what is to be our political Soul;
will we all in the act
become reconciled to
and surpass our past?
Will we move through race, history and beyond
even 20th century capitalism?

Can generations meet
in the between
and give new birth to Hope?

Will granddad's view of the past;
his dislikes and loyalties
reconcile with the children, the young people
whites, blacks, minorities, women, all lined up
at the Body Politic
seeking solace and New Times?
or will they all say: "I know granddad what you think
but I just don't think about it that way."

In every hamlet and one-street town every suburb and city
the lines form and the hearts vote to express what each soul
believes is the best for all of us.

What is Best America?

Send out some white doves to find our soul and let's hope
they come back, after the vote with good news.

There is no forked road here; this feels like a new road.

But, note: hopes aside
demographics plus luck
determine all our fates;

Yes, we can.

We cannot afford to
can not
or not can.

Obama Had Won: Rekindling Hope For A New American Dream;

America Is A Dream: The Night of Dried Tears:

Many cried when the TV said, he'd won. He was just a man but, what a man. It was just an election, but, what an election. But, we all realized that night America is not just another country.

America Is A Dream

In the Rotations
of the Universe
periodically,

the Destiny Dial clicks
to that space
called Community.

Then the entire world
celebrates
and weeps-
tears
which
reflect
each hope,
each dream;

when we all plant
our Heart Seeds
in the garden of
"The Future Which Heals;"

not Miracles
but, maybe Peace,
not Riches;
but more; Shared Prosperity;

not
no fear,
but lessened anxiety.

America is a Dream.

Every once in a while
She produces that hand
which re-lights Lady Liberty's torch
and more light comes;

a new hand reaches out
to millions of other hands
which reach back
affirming the simple
retort:
Yes We Can.

Sing now,
as others have sung,
for phase, line and meter
bring back the music.

only America can sing,
of an era
which maybe,
just maybe
will crack that shut door,

where Hope's light will
shine through
upon child faces

where the children glimpse
new possibilities;
where new shinings
illuminate each child face,
issue new blessings to each
and their progeny;

all bathed now in that precious prospect
where there is respect
for lives human and non-human;

where peace is not extinguished
by flesh-mauling war machines.

American is The Dream
which won't die;

a Liberty Experiment--
amid swarms of tyrannies;
where sometimes
the Universal Clock Pointer
swings round to the Justice Point.

All this
signaled, potentially,
by a goat herder's son
who had that same dream.

Democracy is that system
best preserved,
because no one knows
where Potential
will emanate from;

or lessons that can be learned
from a goats herders son
and that Kansas wife
who had a different dream.

A last one:
Good luck Mr. President

Yes, the tears flow.
A President inaugurates;
Hope rises.
Faith renewed.
Fire comes down
to light the candle
this will show us our way.
Good luck
Mr. President
while the way is long,
we travel it together.

The nights will stretch away
into years
but our writing hand
will not stall
over the difficult parts

History is being written here.
Good luck Mr. President
we are counting on us.

Election Night Was Life and Death For Harriet:

For all the joy there was election night, life did go on for some without surcease. This is Harriet's election night story.

Harriet loved too much, Harriet loved too long. She lived in a marriage of hero-worship. She was the shy bookish girl who ended up marrying the local town banker's son who became a hero to many in her community, saving houses and offering sometimes risky loans: loaning money to farmers for seed, or stock or equipment. He was generally acknowledged to have saved their town and additionally brought in a new Wal-mart, and adding a new industrial park.

But now her husband of 32 years lay dying of cancer, election night, and Harriet after years of devotion to her hero-husband--years of being willing to walk and live in his shadow--wanted only one thing from him-permission to move on after his death. He had asked her if she would remarry if he died and she stammered and didn't answer. He quickly told her not to; it would hurt the children, create confusion over the will and would not look good in the town.

She hadn't answered him then, but, when the hospital called to say he did not have long she went to his side and again asked. She wanted his permission to move on, to start a new life. The dying husband, virtually with his last breath, refused her that permission. Harriet cried at the funeral for many reasons; that was one of them.

But she has respected his wish. She has resigned herself to the life of a lonely widow.

So even as the world, seemingly celebrated, some Americans were did not; change for Harriet was not going to happen, and could not; prevented even beyond the grave. She mentioned that in their bedroom, she has turned her late husband's picture
to the wall.

Harriet represents, in my view, one of the down sides to hero-worship, to excess devotion which refuses to change with the times. It can be negative for those worshipped in this way and for those fixed in that adoration.

The adored, can come to take that adoration for granted, can become self-centered and narcissistic; a danger all politicians face. The roar of the crowd--the fawning is difficult to walk away from. It becomes, as in Harriet's case, a case of supply and demand. Those who thrive on adoration hook-up with those who have a need to supply that adoration. Politicians and their publics can, sometimes, step into that kind of relationship to the detriment of the body politic. I am not predicting Obama has this affliction; I am saying there is always that danger for the adored.

Election Night Babies:

Election night brought America together, brought
disagreements too among families, bought joy for many,
despair for others.

Election night couples reconciled coming together with each
other and with neighbors, with family and some even within
whole neighborhoods. A community feels, the excitement, the
sense that the entire globe was involved providing an emotional
backdrop for the entire nation voting night.

Demographists predict a slew of Obama babies in August,
since lovers loved, reconciled or opened up to each other in this
period perhaps more so than ever.
Babies happen when people start talking.

Katlyn had a story of reconciliation during this period and she
says she got pregnant election night or the night after.

Katlyn's Dawn:

There was, for almost two years, talk about Hope in the air I
guess it permeated everything, politics, marriages and love
affairs. "It did ours," she wrote, "Two of us together" she
noted "make a dull marriage and video games don't really help
pass the time."
"But, Obama kept talking about hope and just maybe it seeped
into our house, into our bedroom, just before dawn, after one
long night."
We were both lying in bed and suddenly he says "I have been
faking it"

I said "me too"
"That was how it started. How we started talking about us, about the marriage; how we had been like kids playing house, no children, just work and movies and video games and camping trips but we didn't really talk about the future, about having kids. I wanted kids; I knew he didn't, so we didn't talk about it. I talked about it with my mom but that is about all, except maybe with my best friend. "

"But that night, election night we talked about Obama; what he would really do. About all his talk about hope and whether that whole thing was just politics. But we did discover our own little brand of hope for our marriage, at least we started."

"Maybe," she thought, "Obama got many people thinking about what they hoped for in life, and some like us acting upon it."

Four months along the baby is healthy and they are going to name him Barry if it is a boy and Michelle if it is a girl. Barry is the name Obama used in his early years.

Now here is another part of the story.

The personal stories of Americans, have for many, become interwoven with the Obama story and this election. Nixon did not have this reaction, not Clinton, not even Reagan. No one probably since Roosevelt.

The idea here is that if Obama can maintain that kind of personal connection with the voters all through his first term, he will get a second term, almost no matter what happens. The magnitude of the crisis is such that allowances will likely be made for him and he will likely be given a second bite at the Presidential apple. After all he is almost family, isn't he?

The African-American Community-Single Parents:

Election night was, of course a special night for African Americans. The group I want to focus on is the single parent American- American family. After all, Obama came from a single parent home.

It was a bad time to be single during the 2008 presidential election. The Obama's had that beautiful family and some single mothers had to explain to their younger children where their Dad was. Unmarried women over 40, especially, had to face the prospect they would never have a woman-man marriage.

Almost 40% of black women never get married, never get proposed to. Mika is typical. She has photos of Obama now in her living room, the first since Jack Kennedy.

One risks mangling metaphors, but my sense is that for some of these women, the election the first black male at the Presidential level they could point to for their children to emulate.

The inauguration, for some of them as well, was a wedding. On election night the nation had proposed to Barack Obama but the wedding ceremony had not taken place. The inauguration was the final step, the walk down the aisle, the taking of the oath-wedding vow, the statement in public of the commitment, the wedding reception after, twenty inaugural balls, prince and–princess are getting married and the whole world will be watching. Mika says that how she felt. Beyonce sang at her wedding. Michelle Obama stood in for her.

The powerful emotional and symbolic content of this upon the black community, especially single women cannot be understated, Here is a community with, a third of the young men in jail, many undereducated and jobless, many gone away to war, gone away taken by drugs or disease. Many of her children growing up fatherless. No father figures to point to, no male figures for her to relate to as she struggles through life. Mika had no prince charming.

She herself was not likely to find her prince charming in all of this familial devastation. But there is Barack, his is not in jail, he got through school, his is the father she can point her kids to, he is the prince charming she too, did not get.

Moreover, he is not the man who when, she becomes pregnant turns out to be just passing through.

Barack is not just passing through, he will be there four, maybe eight years. Most marriages don't last much longer than that.
The point is made.

So What Does The Election Mean?

If hope is on the landscape; and devotion the modality; then
Obama is a phenomenon. Does he have the potential to
become an internalized, a generational icon; a Franklin
Roosevelt, a Reagan?

When a population internalizes a figure they take personally
their hearts; name children after them, put their picture up on
the walls at home along side those of family; talk about them in
daily conversations, talk about them in church, draw
confidence from daily reports of what they are doing, speak of
them with pride, then, internalization has occurred.

With this kind of internalization, the figure in question rises to
a level of being beyond question; can do no wrong. their being
there is subsistence enough, they are beyond question, beyond
criticism; they are their own reason for being, beyond
reproach.
For some in the black community Obama can, and for some,
has already has reached that stage. They now fear that others
will tarnish that view of him; that assassination is always on
the horizon as a danger. Obama is seen as their person, to be
protected as a family member would be protected against that
which would undermine him and his efforts.

This, coupled with other groups and their sentiments similar to
this has, as it's outcome, generational loyalty.
A whole generation focused on one person as their icon. Of
course, the democrats hope that that loyalty will rub off on the
party as well. Perhaps it will, perhaps it won't, but the point is

that Barack Obama just might command that stature irrespective of the party component.

In political matters we often ask why do people vote the way they do We have identified class, habit, family and other reasons, but the ones I think were dominant in this election were three: wallet issues; ideological issues and heart issues.

When a politician reaches heart level, the realties of economics or ideology don't matter. The heart never relinquishes what it has chosen to love.

It is this period between election and the inauguration, I call the middle passage. This was a critical period. The initial euphoria or dread if you opposed Obama, all comes to take more permanent form in this middle period.
For example, for some Obama moved from glee at this success to become an internalized part of the lives and their psyche during the middle period.
For those concerned with wallet issues he was being given control over their wallet, indeed their future, Some were hopeful about that-- some were and are fearful. For those wedded to policy and ideological consideration, he, in this period, becomes a dangerous "socialist" or he is throwing ideology aside in favor of getting something done.

My point is that these stances solidify in that middle period, election to inauguration. Of the three, the most unassailable and difficult to change, is the internalization outcome.

Below is an example of how the three interplay.
My company raised money for the victims of the Hurricane. Grateful, I heard from the executive director of a group we benefited. She complained that years later New Orleans was forgotten. Promises of money and support were broken and the governor was refusing money that the Obama administration was offering.

She was clear though that even if the Obama administration fared no better that the Bush administration on delivering on promises that Obama's popularity would not be affected, He was not being judged in the minority communities of New Orleans on wallet or ideological grounds, "they have taken the man into their hearts and once there it don't matter what he does or doesn't do within reason."

Internalization gives Obama more time, more support, and the internalized strength which will make a second run far easier.

After the Election and Before the Inaugural—Middle Period Jobs:

After the election, and before the Inauguration, the euphoria gathers momentum for some and the jockeying for jobs in the new administration begins in earnest.
Hope baskets, metaphorically, were piling higher and higher in front of the White House gates.

But the world, from the standpoint of ordinary Americans, did not stand still. They were not going to get one of those plumb administration jobs; they were not going to be on TV talking about the future of the economy.
They were having to go back to work, to carry on as usual. They were not going to get one the one hundred and forty thousand jobs a new President has to fill. But right away, a new President, especially a President Obama has to face the dilemmas and contradictions between running as candidate and running a government.

This middle period between the election and Inauguration is where the chickens come home to roost—all over those 144 thousand jobs. What chickens?
The issue becomes who, and what criteria, will the new president use to fill those jobs; political loyalty, cronyism, equality opportunity principles, merit, or affirmative action precepts?

Transcendent values in American history and politics are involved here; Equality, Freedom, Justice and Merit.

Here are the dilemmas:

Appoint former lobbyists? The campaign had centered around clearing the lobbyists out of politics and influence in American government. To turn around and appoint them in large numbers would have political ramifications. Obama compromised and allowed waivers for some positions and allowed former lobbyists and individuals with lobbyist ties to be appointed. Compromise.

Continue the old Chicago school of politics and appoint friends and supporters to positions as a reward for their support, especially if it was early support and included large donations or cash bundling? Obama did try to reward friends coupled with a political calculus: appoint friends and supporters who could also be helpful with re-election. Richardson of New Mexico comes to mind. But that misfired because if that person appears to violate precepts of equality, justice, fairness then the appointment will falter and did. Richardson, and a possible contract scandal in New Mexico, would remind voters too much of Chicago-style politics and hurt Obama and his vow not to do politics that way.

Therefore, the politics of who gets what when where and how had to be abandoned in favor merit-based appointments or at least the appearance of such.

But merit, as a basis for government appointments, vs. a spoils Chicago-style system, reflects a long history of tension between the two. All presidents have appointed with a mixture of the two. Obama is largely doing the same. However, he has added the additional problem of having proclaimed he would not do crony politics, but the practical fact is that he needs the

support of his supporters and they want jobs in the new administration.
Civil Rights and Equality vs. Merit based politics.

Another dilemma looms. Supporters from minority communities strongly supported Obama and many expected jobs as a reward.

However, Obama preached merit; he is the merit based African-American whose life said you can make it if you work hard.

The Civil Rights movement, and many of its leaders, came at the issue from another vantage point. Their position was and continues to be that the Obama's of the world are anomalies and cannot be placed forward as examples of a merit based system. The race starts out unequally and it does not matter that one or two individuals succeed; this only highlights the fact that the situation for the many does not change.

Obama's retort is that change has to come to the many and that means uplifting the middle class. Hence, post racial politics also means that government has to be merit-based to be effective.

Affirmative action, equality-based principles, pleas for special consideration for past injustices, fly in the face of the bread and butter issue of who will get a merit-based loyalty rewarding government appointment.

Put starkly Obama has the sharpest dilemma of any modern President. He is squarely fastened to the horns of that dilemma; one where the issue is will he disappoint those who gave him 90-95% support in his bid for election—the African-American community, or give those jobs to white Americans on the basis of merit?

African-Americans, women and minorities are already concluding that they have not been adequately rewarded. Obama cannot ignore this complaint and still hope for re-election.

Tough dilemma.

Tough because equality issues are wrapped up with justice issues. If I start out in poverty, I never get the education, I therefore, never get the job, and therefore, never get the experience and hence, a self-perpetuating spiral is created.

Even if gains are made they can be dashed in the next bubble crash. Millions of Americans poor and middle classes have effectively been driven back down, at bargain prices into the lower middle class or blocked from mobility where homes, their major asset, are being sold at bargain basement prices.

This has generational ramifications. Lacking an economic base these families won't be able to afford college, some might become homeless or deplete their savings and it will take years to make up losses from the 401k debacle.

Therefore, the size of an under-class grows and grows in America. Children will carry forth the story of how the family lost the house, couldn't afford college or lost half or most of their savings due to the greed on Wall Street. The echoes will go on even if there is a mild recovery. So the appointment process pits merit against justice in the context of shrinking resources.

Finally, the traditional leaders of the African American community have built a movement based upon precepts of Equality and Justice and Affirmative action. Obama does not share those precepts. He represents a new generation with precepts skewed more toward those of freedom of action, individual imitative, and organizing among middle class whites--merit precepts.

This is a clash not only of generations but will bring to the surface the clashes between these precepts long embedded in American political history and their attendant unresolved tensions.

These date from the days of Andrew Jackson to the present.

They are so pervasive we Americans don't notice them. A quick example: How does the notion of the equality of every individual square with a work a day world which is based upon hierarchy, control and job-holders that are "ruled" over by a boss.

They don't mesh very well at all and American history is replete with attempts to democratize organizations, town-hall meetings, and the caucus system of voting--all designed to maximize the equality maxim.

They have not worked very well because equality clashes with freedom of action. The right to succeed in the race trumps the value of starting the race on an equal footing. Americans and their immigrant ancestors came to America to get rich and escape the equality of slaves, serfs and subjects of the old world.

This short piece below makes the point.

I'll Take Freedom With a Side of Justice and Equality To Go:

This undercurrent in American political and social life is now boiling. Obama's successful candidacy high-lights what was, always conflicts, among cherished American precepts of Liberty, Equality, Justice, Civil Rights and notions of Freedom.

He represents the post-civil rights generation. Rights proponents from the women's movement, gays, and immigrants have a conundrum: demanding equal access to a system which you have condemned in other discussions.

Moreover, there is the slave's dilemma outlined below. What is best—Equality, Freedom or Justice and who decides?

A Slave's Chronicle

Justice?

Let me tell you something about Justice-
the kind that smells funny and never comes.

The Justice of the Wronged
never sees the light of day

Justice is following the rules
and laws made by others.

Justice is begging to be treated
like all the rest of the slaves,

and then being asked "why aren't you satisfied"?

Justice is pretending that because a judge said it,
that makes it just.

It doesn't.

Judge Justice is just us pretending that better to be ruled by
judges and majorities than by a dictator's whims.

What difference does that make?

Why do 51 get to rule over 49?
Where is the justice in that?

Where is the democracy in that?
No where, that's where.

Don't need me no Justice.
Don't need me no Equality.

What I need
is me some Freedom.

After I say that
the room
gets all quiet.

Ain't No Equality or Freedom, or Justice at Work:

The above points clearly to the work place. Americans grapple with these contractions everyday. They are not academic.

Work Place, Equality and Freedom

"We struggle with it under many names;
we all feel the tension and the tug- how can I as a child
learn equality and go to work where equality dies in the
bureaucracy- a lonely stepchild?

Where in the hierarchical schema chart does Freedom live?

Where is Justice--in the work place Staff Meeting?

No, we all have bosses and contemplate each day
where do my child-learned ideals fit?

I will tell you; in the Water Cooler Gossip Group.

There is where Justice is done; complaints are vent,
where equality before the H2O is talked about and dispensed.

How can what I learned as democracy be banned from my
work space?

How can Fairness and Morality be slaughtered like the lamb
in the hierarchy?

We have revolutions not because of the ruling class
but, because of the anger exposed and felt before the Water-
Cooler Deity; where shock and awe exist; plots and plannings
mint, from the latest gossip-tidbit to strategic strategies shared
among participants who like soldiers and couriers make sure
to dispense each bon mot and redemption amid far and wide
alertings to those who did not make the morning Water-Cooler
Meet.

True community exists here, at this Water Cooler Church
complete with the Paper Water Cooler Communion Cup.
Drink up-the Salvation Coming.

Truths long concealed bubble up; Truthiness is clear like
Evian; we drink it down and steeled, return to that cubicle
space for another run at Demon Boss who hovers overhead;
the Lufiwaulfe; verbal bombs and critiques, bomb bay opened-
-ready for release.

Excuse me I need a drink. Can't stand too much more
of this Equality."

Obama has that this and other perceptual problems to a
greater degree than any President in recent memory. How he
fares in resolving these in his governing style remains to be
seen.

For sure it will not be easy. For sure some will be disappointed
and a reaction will occur. The Obama plan is to satisfy enough
of the electorate at the same time simultaneously, moving to his
Presidency to the internalization state to get some things done
and to get re-elected.

But there is another force relevant to Obama's chances of getting re-elected. That is the media.

Obama and the Media: His Future May Depend Upon the Media-True or False?

Selling the idea of Hope, and even Democracy, propounded by a black politician from corrupt Chicago was more than much of the media could stomach.

Media Storms and False Bluster:

For young people who paid attention to the press and media coverage of the election, the contentiousness, seemed at times seemed overwhelming. The adult world appeared scary to some of them who were unsteadied by the vitriol which came pouring into living rooms across the nation. They watched the Daily Show where the political news came with a bit of humor instead.

But make no mistake this election was a media event-a media bonanza.

"The Right could raise hundreds millions pitching "Obama is coming with his terrorists friends and he is not one of us pitch;" the Left had "lets take the country back and elect a black man—wouldn't that be special?" message. Commentators and pundits whip-lashed listeners and watchers with daily atrocity stories to pump up ratings and to get candidate "A" to spend money in the media to counter the overnight claims of candidate "B."

Conservative media operations condemned Obama while making millions off politicians--democrats and republicans-- who bought air time; off drug and conservative groups who bought politicians to defend the status quote. The politicians had it easy: whip up the constituency and tell them to donate to your campaign, whip up the Right or the Left special interests and tell them to donate to your campaign; go on TV and help with their ratings—so they make more money, some of which you expect to get back in donations.

It's all about money... for everyone involved. There are no virgins here. Obama raised more money but who got that money—the same conservative special interest media conglomerates he condemned? He tried to raise money from small donations but it was not enough. Everyone got money from wall street and what a coincidence Wall Street got billions in bail out money.

Its all about money. Is that too cynical?

The tabloidization of media in the United States is rampant, driven in part by shrinking revenues in print media especially. Newspapers, TV, Radio, even the internet are all in cut back mode.

A presidential election can represent 25% of the entire revenue for the year for some media outlets. Presidential campaigns are crucial to the bottom line.

There is, however, less news; rather we get phony atrocity scare stories and gossip; we get reporters interviewing reporters both getting pay checks from the same boss conglomerate; we get distractions, reality shows, Jerry

Springer-like amusements, so we don't interfere with the folks really running the important things which effect our lives.

Think: where were the media in examining the Iraq war, in examing the Bush torture sessions, civil liberties erosions, the environment?

They were all feeding from the Washington money-trough while the middle class in the United States was being sold out, jobs sent overseas, while whole industries were being abandoned and being told all of this was good for America.

But it wasn't. Wall street collapses, life savings disappear and the plan is keep it going after modest reforms.

The old Whoopi Goldberg quote is a good one—paraphrasing.

"You don't mind getting mugged in a bad neighborhood, all they get in your wallet; but don't go anywhere near Wall Street—they rob you of your life-savings and your future"

All of this is ongoing in the context of increasing tabloidization of media and segmentation into markets; conservative radio stations, liberal radio stations, print media, broadcast media all fragmented and segmented--all commanding audiences which never have to hear a dissenting view--audiences which can be prompted to send money and support candidates after their segment has been hyped by the fragmented media.

Cross over media that is media which talks to a wide audience is becoming more and more rare.

More and more Americans are listening to fewer and fewer media and only to those individuals and media which agree with their political and social points of view.

This is not compatible with Democracy which assumes a free press, that free speech results in exposure to a wide variety of points of view—an informed public.

After the Election—After Media—Harm or Help?

The role of the media does not end with the election.

It will continue throughout the tenure of the administration. The point is that the media will go where dollars and ratings lead. There is the attempt to capture audience and those of similar opinion and hope they watch, listen to, or read only your media outlet.

Pandering and leading has a very slim line drawn between them, but the acid test is that these are for-profit companies.

Few can survive on purely ideological grist if they are losing large dollars. Some survive as small outlets but they lack the financial resources to have national impact.

So the media will change as they sense Obama's fortunes change.

But note that despite the attempts of many media outlets to lead opinion about Obama, the media, over-all, and their pundits were relatively ineffective in changing the over-all results of the election.

Obama's average of the polls remained steady thought out despite media polls designed to show him ahead by 15 points to rally the troops or behind by 15 points to rally the troops.

In the end the American people showed themselves to be pretty savvy in evaluating media messages and pundit offers of wisdom. They ignored them.

But the media are always there. They played their role during the election, and during the transition and now in the Obama Presidency. Any President has to manage the media and the only defense is continuously high approval ratings which have been internalized for significant voting population groups.

But let's pick up the thread after the transition period has been completed. Transition period completed—what's next?

Post Inauguration and Obama's Big Ideas:

Hope.

A change election brings to the fore the question of change from what to what?
Obama, in trying to forge his image and his ideas, stirred interest as to what key ideas in his campaign actually mean and the place of these same key ideas and their meanings in American History.

What are Obama's big ideas and their meanings?

The campaign talked a lot about hope but, of course, hope was not specifically defined. Hope is about change, and, we understand, hope is about a better future; about leaving behind the worse things from the past for a better future. But again, what is hope?

Among my readers, of course, a lively discussion ensued as to what is hope anyway? And what does the dictionary say it is? What been the history of hope's definition over the years, over the centuries?

"Never was a larger word
than Hope;
all dreams reside there."
                    Quote from Poem "What is Hope" Lonnie Hicks

Hope, it seems has several variations in its meanings. Hope can be based upon expectations; an expectation that I will achieve some goal or attain some dream or desire.

But what are these expectations, in turn, based upon? And how is hopes opposites--failure, despair and disappointment to be avoided? What is to be the pivotal aspect of hope which will ensure success?

Well, we quickly grasp that nothing is guaranteed in the hoping. Failure is always an option and often is the most likely outcome for all our hoping. But we go on hoping and dreaming doesn't we?

Why?

Well, apparently hope has a Leap of Faith component; and a sense of gambling that, against the odds, the future we want to see occur will actually occur despite the odds.

But faith in what? Is this religious faith, faith in God, in one own capacities and potential, in probabilities?

Cave men had faith that leaving Africa for the unknown would work out. But faith supplied by what? No God, no church was there for them. Theirs must have been a true leap of faith, a tremendous form for dreaming for a better life and striking out to make it happen.

This faith itself does not require an explanation. It is its own justification which is ultimately mysterious—even as it has been shown to be effective. People hope, dream and act upon those hopes and dreams and make things happen. Happens everyday.

But we are asking what is to be the ultimate outcome from the leap of faith Obama is asking the American public to make?

Obama and we are now embarking upon a journey where the fate of America-- indeed the fate of many nations may hinge.

Believing in something, not probable, not even rational is the basis of the entire human enterprise. That is the value of faith, leaping or otherwise.

By what rational exercise did a goat-headers son from Kenya hope that his son would be President of the United States? No rule to account for that.

Now we have come full circle. Barack Obama is a living example of a leap of faith. He embodies and puts the anti-hope model to shame. An outcome is an outcome. His dad hoped against the odds and his son became President of the United States.

So what is the hope of the future is Obama actually offering; what is its basis?

The child of hope is now, naturally asking another leap of faith in him, in government action to fix health care, to fix the financial system, to fix America. He is a product of hope and naturally he believes in its power to overcome all obstacles.

But note here the twist. Obama's hope is really the organizers hope: that a mobilized America, millions strong, can over come. This is the essence the democratic faith and credo: leaders have no answers without an informed, mobilized public behind them. That is, at base, the Obama strategy. The odds of success are maximized the more minds, and energies, are brought to bear upon the issues and problems.

And who are we to say he's wrong yet? We have to wait and see.

Happiness: A Corollary of Hope:

But what good is hope if we don't also imagine that having our dreams come true will also result in making us happy?

So what does it mean to be happy? Personal happiness—when things are happy in our lives, when we are pleased with our selves, our circumstances or in our families, community, and nation—is this happiness?

But hoping that every single person in the world will be happy is clearly unattainable so do we mean most people being happy? Which people? Who is it ok to let be unhappy?

Happiness, it turns out, is not so easy to define. But that did not stop the dictionary makers from trying. So what do they have to say about the definition of happiness and it's history?

Happiness, it turns out is not guaranteed no matter what you do. Happiness is part luck, part fate, and we, in life, are only promised its pursuit, not its guarantee.

So if hope is my driver then happiness note is not guaranteed such that our hopes and dreams will end in happiness.

Happiness is derived from the word hap which means luck.

Hapless is to be unlucky.

There is some hard truth here. Hope alone is no guarantee, and even if it were an iron clad component of everyone's thoughts and actions, happiness as a result of all this effort, on hope's behalf are not a guaranteed outcome?

Apparently, relating back to Obama, the world has so many variables which effect outcomes; no guarantees, therefore, are possible; and moreover, there is no one, or no one government which has the ability to control all the relevant variables.

No one man, no one person is smart enough, bluntly put, to figure out that plan.

Collectively, perhaps, a plan can emerge. But that implies full engagement of everyone's mind and thoughts.

And this by the way is the rationale for Democracy. Engage the minds of all the citizens because no one leader or set of leaders is smart enough to run everything.

And, interesting enough Obama's message is the same. "We are the ones we have been waiting for. Don't count on me, count on us."

In the end hope is based on the Democratic notion that while nothing is guaranteed in this life, we maximize our changes at success by fully engaging the support, ideas and energies of all citizens. That is the message of Democracy and it is all the credo of the community organizer Barack Obama.

What Is To Be The New Definition of Progress-Obama style?

Well now given some clarity on hope, Democracy and the American brand of happiness, what is to be the impact of these ideas on the traditional American faith in unending progress toward bigger and better things?

What now is to be the definition of progress given the shocks to the financial, political, and social systems world wide?

Americans are doubting the definition of Progress. Is it the restoration of the old polluting industrial base? Will the new green economy result is higher taxes, one step up and two steps back?
Is the American dream practical anymore?

Should I be learning Chinese?

Progress?

There was this struggling;
a knife-sharp shovel blade
dug deep in Earth's rib-cage;

tall tree limbs severed
which drop to the ground;
habitant homes invaded
and brook arteries polluted;
by drugs and poisons.

The warming eye of sun-
blinded by carbon rain
and stinging neon gas-
make sun-sets
and sun downs
red red red.

The animals
flee
to hovels
beneath
the shrinking ground
and pavements slather
on more and more concrete.

Mountains recede
worn down;
the ocean waters
rise to heal the scars
to take back the
dusty dry lands.

Smoke stacks
and coal pits;
Nuclear plants
and nuclear fission.

All this
as the Earth sheds
a near final tear,
weeping
asking:
is this
Progress?

Certainly the old definition of progress: bigger and better, endless growth in production, in incomes; in output looks a little unrealistic.

The bubble burst this time and the bathtub disappeared too.

What Is To Be The New Paradigm?

The new definition of progress has not yet been fully articulated but there are some scattered ideas Obama has spoken to.
The new economy will have several new measures of progress;
It will be non-polluting with a green manufacturing base;
It will be education-driven and presumably geared toward supplying the brains for the new green economy;
It will be one where markets will have more regulation, enough to prevent the collapse we are currently witnessing;
It will be less American consumer driven; other countries will have to take on their fair load in terms of stabilizing the world economy;
It will be less fossil-fuel dependent;
It will be aimed squarely at restoring the purchasing power of the American middle class;
It will build the infrastructure needed for economic supports;
It will reform government costs, including Medicare, Social Security and Health care Costs;
It will reduce American expenditures on Military Hardware;
It will move toward a more global approach to economics as opposed to an American dominated global system;
It will be a new global economy based on the productive capacity of emerging nations.;
It will be an economy moving more toward providing national service utilizing the energies of young people to help move the American economy in these new directions;

We ask what is the likelihood that these ambitious plans will work?
My view: as yet unknown, but my suspicion is that they will not.

The above plans and notions are too little too late, too expensive, too much opposition, too impractical and not enough time, or brain power to implement even a few of them-- and worse--they are all so interconnected all of them have to be done for one of them to succeed.

Last, all of them call for a degree of central planning and control no one man or group of people have the brains to do; too massive, too convoluted and not likely to succeed as outlined above.

But let's go to detail on some of the Obama agenda and take a closer look at the challenges and why change is so difficult.

Obama's Plans and Their Challenges--The Financial Crisis: Buddy, Can You Spare a Few Trillion?

The collapse of the financial system has created consternation world wide. As this is written, many of the sentiments from an earlier piece still apply: how to restore the public, indeed world faith, in the capitalist system while making the necessary reforms to keep a similar collapse from re-occurring.

Not an easy task. But what is the nature of the system to be reformed? The key issue is that if free markets do not operate as they are supposed to, if financial institutions get too big to fail then what can or does change mean?

What does it mean to be too big to fail?

Conglomeration in the twenty century comes in many flavors not just those relating to the financial systems. It is a world wide conglomeration, different than the robber baron system of the 19th century. This one a winding web of nterdependence and, as it turns out, of collapse.

First, let look at the military industrial complex Eisenhower warned about. The United States has over 714 military bases around the world. Why? Aside from the usual imperialism answers the brute fact is that these bases are integral parts of the economies where they are located.

It is and will be extremely difficult to close these bases, since much of even European prosperity, is based on not having to pay for their own defense; since many weapons systems are manufactured in these countries where they form an important part of those economies.

We cannot easily close military bases in the United States either because whole communities depend upon the bases upon the weapons system built there. In bad times do you want to exacerbate matters by increasing military related unemployment?

Military families, veterans all depend upon the military budget. Veterans living under viaducts, homeless veterans on the streets-is not politically acceptable.

Besides, like World War I vets, they could easily get the guns and march on Washington.

The military and military arms sales are a significant source of revenue for the United States. Other countries that protect American interests abroad have to be given arms to perform that defense function. Especially oil related functions protecting oil supplies and routes. Interrupt that supply and American industry, goes into chaos, all things bad will happen if there were to be an interruption in the flow of oil.

We have little choice but to defend the oil supply lines.

So, we have a military, industrial, defense and financial global system which indeed is inter-related and put another way, a house of cards—all supported by American dollars, by American blood and by American consumption.
Now all three are in jeopardy.

The American financial system has as a similar dilemma. Banks take in American dollars and loan those same dollars back to Americans at inflated credit card interest rates. In the latest credit freeze why don't banks lend out the money they have, and whose money is it anyway?

Americans in the end, being denied access to funds the banks got from Americans in the first place and these same banks insist that Congress give them more American dollars to release the ones they already have.

This is a hostage system, and this intentional or unintentional blackmail is one which reveals a terrible weaknesses. The big banks and insurance companies are too big to fail. They must be rescued to some extent or the whole system could and almost did collapse.

Promises to fix all this with new regulations sound a bit hollow. Will trillions in bail-out monies create a new fail-safe financial system? No one thinks so. Nor do I.

Health care looms as another huge user of the GNP (Gross National Product.) Health care costs grow at 10% a year while GNP languishes with flat or even negative growth. Medicare, the hospital system is an expensive system but is an entitlement program. Do we through Grandma out in the streets? No.

Private and employer paid health care plans all have flaws in the "lets try to fix them scenario:" tinker with them and they could collapse before we have anything to replace them; tinker and huge opposition will arise—almost insurmountable opposition; tinker and you'll soon find there is really precious little money available to work with.

Ditto, on the infrastructure needs of the country, ditto on cleaning up the water, ditto on climate change and what will be necessary to really be effective in all of this.

So what way is out?

Well, the American consumption engine is done. We are eyeball level in debt and no new industries to bail us out.

So the IMF (International Monetary Fund) gets billions because the emerging nations have to be looked to as new drivers of consumption. Here is China, here is India, and here is Latin America. They have to bail the west of this mess and their economies are not so centralized so as to be a danger world wide. Fragmented economies are a plus in this environment.

Therefore plank one in any world wide recovery plan will have to include replacing the American consumer driver with the consumption driver from emerging economies.

So aside from emerging economies what else offers a possible way out?

We could look, as Obama suggests look to green industry as the wedge to the future, Green cut expensive pollution, could provide the jobs of the future; could create competitive new technologies to give America a new competitive advantage. But that will take education and American students don't do the heavy sciences.

Foreign students dominate in the sciences, especially at the graduate student level. Where will the brains for the American revival come from?

All of this could be overwhelmed by external unplanned for events like a major disease out-break; unexpected global warming occurrences, threats to the water supply, a terrorist attack that cripples an important causeway or city.

Many of these, aside from the lost of life potentially involved, can also prove to be expensive.

And, with the increasing, seemingly ineffectiveness of society to respond to these hypothetical threats we will see, if history, is a guide, increasing demands upon government to do something.

We can expect too a rise in millennialism and end of times thinking; the belief that we are in the end times and the world will see the rise of the ant-Christ, or the second coming. We will likely see food and water riots. Not possible? I wouldn't be to sure.

America grocers have only five days supplies of food on their shelves. Cut the supply and people will take matters into their own hands.

So green energy and the restoration of the manufacturing base in the United States does not seem feasible at any reasonable price.

A green economy assumes a work force is available, highly educated in the sciences, plentiful and cheap. These are not in place and won't be for many years.
Scratch the green economy model.

The race to develop new and cheat sources of food, of energy, of labor is a race against time. These have been alluded to by Obama policy makers.

Countries need to grow, provide food, cheap energy and cheap labor in order to supply jobs and livelihoods to its citizens or risk social upheaval.

War in the past has been an outcome where resources are essentially taken by force by one country from another country.

While war in not a permanent answer to economic woes we have found that, in fact, war offers a temporary boost to economic development. Things get blown up and have to be replaced often. This produces jobs. War also means access one's enemy's natural resources. And as with Nazi Germany, we see that cheap labor in the form of labor camps was important to Germany's ability to prosecute the war. Ugly picture but that is how history tells us cheap labor, cheap energy and cheap food have been pillars of societies. They are often seized in war.

What is different is this era, is, of course, the specter of nuclear weapons. All bets are off here, All strategies pale with the nuclear threat. Nothing which can be built cannot be destroyed by nuclear weapons used in war or otherwise.
Let's have a look at nuclear weapons and how their emergence effect all out best plans outlined above.

The Nuclear Option Trumps All Other Options:

Military leaders, could in the past, tell their populations that they could be protected by military might. Not so in this nuclear era. One nation could have a rouge colonel set off nuclear explosions and the fallout could drift around the world, ruining water supplies, creating radiation sickness in millions, creating new disease outbreaks thereby creating a world crisis which could be horrendous.

What is startling about the 9-11 attack is that it nearly brought down huge segments of the American economy with five airplanes. Interdependcy here is a weakness, not a strength. So what is to be done? Can anything be done? Well maybe.

What Will Be Obama's Governing Style in Crisis Mode?

Before we move to speculation on solution-sets for these huge issues let have a look at what is likely to be the Obama style in dealing with the myriad decisions he will have to make as President pursing solutions. How he governs is material to any postulated successes the administration might enjoy.

We ask what will likely the Obama be governing style given what we have postulated about his political origins. Moreover, what will be the pros and cons of that style matched against problems he will face as President?

Some these issues surfaced in the campaign and we see now, with the concrete problem of governing what his emerging style looks like. Of course, having the job of President changes pre-conceived candidate notions. Obama will not likely be an exception to this rule. But here goes.

Compromise; Pro's and Con's:

While Obama has that steely determination to stay the course he also has the practical streak that says compromise. The question is which will dominate his decision-making on the big issues he faces?

My view is that compromise, on the domestic front, clearly dominates the early months of his Presidency. His background tells us why. He is multi-racial; race enmity is not something he is comfortable with, post partisanship is not a ploy, Obama has that faith that things can be worked out if everyone gets involved. This is after all, the organizers credo and faith.

But the blind spot here is that when individuals and groups see their core issues or lives threatened, they will not compromise.

Sometimes you have to steam-roller issues through and not pause to compromise. Obama has not done that. Rather he has let others do the work while he holds back to forge the final compromise at the end. But note: he does not take the lead on issues from inception to his signing a piece of legislation into law. The rationale, and an understandable one, is that he has some much on his plate he cannot devote the time to every legislative piece. "The perfect should not be the enemy of the good" has been his motto.

He is not making the compromises, congressional deal-makers are making the compromises and he comes in the end to put the final touches on important legislation. This tactic works as long as the details are not crucial to success. If they are Obama's success as president lies in those details and he must engage.

Good enough" progress may get him re-elected but may come at the expense having passed into law programs whose effectiveness is dubious.

Currently this compromise proclivity is being spun as a comparison of his low-key mid-western approach with that of Bush and McCain; non-confrontational but effective governing style.

He is building that image in foreign policy especially. In this area, Obama knows a non-confrontational black President wins kudos among white leaders, and among leaders of color around he world. He has good things going for him with that approach; Cuba. Latin America, Muslim America, emerging countries,
Europe. This tactic has paid dividends so far.

But overall we see what we see with any President: caution in the first term in order to maximize her or her chances at re-election.

Finally, the counter weight to the compromise and "weak" image Obama has under taken is his over-all governing style, designed to move him above criticism and directly bonding with Americans on the psychological level really working?

The point here is that this tack is the only true Teflon place of safety. He knows that being accepted as a member of the family, puts him above criticisms and perhaps even above failure. He knows that daily communication; being in the living rooms of Americans every night helps with that goal. He is showing the American public how hard he is working. He wants his photo on the wall in every home along side family.

He is, in effect, sending letters home every day, letting supporters know what he is doing in the big city. This provides insulation and so, as of this writing, it has worked to keep his approval ratings high. But obviously this will not last and will at the very least ebb and flow.

War And Peace—What will be the Obama Style?

Bad times heighten the potential for war. Nations confronting food riots, energy shortages, unemployment, the collapse of the world financial system, will adopt plans to protect themselves from population reactions which can de-stabilize whole regions, legitimate governments, and vital oil and resource supplies around the world.

This does not take into consideration free-lance criminal gangs, terrorists groups and ideologues who act on their own.

Obama is clearly inclined toward the peace end of the spectrum in so far as government action is concerned. He'd rather not fight. He has focused on nuclear and arms reductions because he clearly sees that as an ultimate threat; he has pushed for green technologies, infrastructure energy use controls, education and cost reductions in health care, Medicare, Social Security and the like. He has plowed billions into wall street and tried to do something for foreclosure-threatened homeowners.

But he undoubtedly knows all this will not be enough. He is not prepared for war and an outcome of any continued severe recession or world wide depression. He has not even spoken of that as a possible consequence of the financial collapse. He doesn't like the topic and that is a weakness of loving peace but not preparing for war. You have to do both.

Internal Controls and Governing:

Much has been written about the Obama management style. Simply put he thinks everyone is like himself, thoughtful, industrious, determined, straight forward, prepares for every contingency and willing to be honest with the boss. He has gone out of his way to appoint aggressive and presumably honest cabinet members and advisors.

That is laudable. But aggressiveness does not necessarily mean that the speaker is your friend and is being honest.
How to know the difference will be important as the administration reels in crisis after crisis. If there comes to be the whiff of failure the aggressive advisors will also be just as aggressive in putting the blame on Obama. Leaks and betrayals will occur. Will Obama, peace-lover, and compromiser surface or will it be the Obama of Chicago politics, quick to the knife and drama-less head rolling. He can do both but which will he do?
A crucial component of all the answers to the Obama enigma and, hence world stability, will lie not in the answers given (note these change daily) but in the final questions identified as central to success. Not answers; but questions. So far the questions being asked are not encouraging. How can the banking system be stabilized; his actions assumes that changes will be minimum and that the only questions are reform questions.

How can new regulation prevent collapses of this kind from reoccurring? Regulation assumes only minimum change.

Taxing carbon emissions? This assumes a continuing pattern of emissions and incremental reductions due to rising costs. First of all companies will not pay the tax they will pass it on to consumers who really right now don't need that burden. If the government insists upon the tax, companies move themselves and jobs overseas.

You can see the issues here.

Here is a mild rant on these topics.
After I go into some of what I consider the right questions which should be asked.

So, I Think I Have the Question, Hold Your Answers:

There are huge question marks around the economy, war and peace, joblessness, finances and the future, all highlighting a political scene where daily new answers are offered from every quarter. This mild rant below was inspired by my academic colleagues who tired of answers without questions.

A Question Anyone?

We have in life
a surfeit
of those who step to the mark
to declare
what should and can be done.

Ideas pour
from their open mouths
enunciating in grave tones
and solemn decrees
making claim
to the Wisdom
of the Knowledge Tree.

Regard these not
or follow those
who claim Secret Lore
and urge "follow me."

Hard Truth:
Every one claims answers
but cannot tell you what is the question;

every one thinks their answer
if true for them
is also true for you;
from that silly stance recoil.

Every sage can tell you what to do
but none can identify the first step.
All can see the path to follow
but none can answer
if a first step
is consistent with several paths which may follow.

None can answer.
If you deny their answers offered,
which are commonly either or choices,
but, note life most often does not show either/or
most often the answer is neither/other.

None can tell you what is scientific about the scientific method.

None can separate in a simple sentence the difference between
book learning and common sense.

No sage alive can claim to know why Progress Now
has crashed so low-despite all the Smart Ones
gone before.

Why is it that ignorance always fills the void
that Knowledge leaves?

Why are there always a surplus of answers
but few good questions?

I don't know
but I know what I don't know
hopefully,
that makes me one step ahead
of those who know the answer
before the question.

Question Anyone?

So we highlight the point: Before we identify answers we must
first ask what are the really important questions to ask?
Well asking new questions is not so easy. If the questions are
really new then the vocabulary for change or for new questions
does not exist and if you insist on creating that new vocabulary
you risk sounding mysterious, or a crack-pot or merely
incomprehensible.

So what to do?

New language to express new ideas is never easy and because
of it vagueness much of what is trying to get expressed has to
be taken on faith. That is what Obama did with the concept of
hope. Vague but people took it and believed it, or gave it a
chance because they believed in Obama.

So new words, new ideas can get implemented by virtue of a
people's faith in their leaders. Obama did just this. But he has
no really new ideas. His plans have a few new goals but they
are not very practical and very expensive.

He has no really new paradigm here rather it is a tightening up of the old paradigm hoping that a reoccurrence of the financial collapse will not occur again.

So real changes in social, political structures can be initiated by leadership but can not succeed except by extraordinary efforts and some luck and the mobilization of large sectors of the population.

Obama's Greatest Challenge-Certainty in The Age of Uncertainty:

Whatever the plans, schemas and goals, the outcome the American public wants above all is certainty. The nation, the globe wants certainty, stability and predictability.

However, this century has been bequeathed uncertainty as its heritage from the last century. Einstein, and Quantum Physics has made it clear that aside from the uncertainties that atomic destruction can bring, we have been put on notice that the fabric our universe, both at the cosmological and the sub-atomic level is uncertain. Electrons pop in and out of existence. Few elements in the periodic table we learned in high school are really stable at the sub-atomic level. Our universe maybe one of many operating in the same space and time as other universes.

Therefore, certainty is gone forever, conceptually speaking. We are now in the world of probabilities, where outcomes cannot be assured but only given impetus to a more probable outcome.

This is the credo of Democracy and it ultimate justification and its greatest enemy. The desire for certainty is so strong populations can become war-like and indeed threaten the planet as a result in its pursuit.

Mussolini promised to make the trains run on time and that was enough for him to gain support for his fascist state. Hitler promised the certainty of a thousand year Reich. History has many examples.

Obama has the problem now that, as an iconic leader, he is trying to lower expectations of perfect certainty while at the same time maintaining his iconic status long enough to get re-elected.

The problem is no one can guarantee that certainty and iconic leaders are often succeeded by a leader promising that certainty so craved by many in the electorate. No one is entirely happy with the future being described as approximate and uncertainty. Markets, peoples, countries,--all will not abide that outcome suggestion.

Therefore, even in the pursuit of probable outcomes, sufficing outcomes, good enough outcomes, not perfect ones, what are Obama's chances of delivering or meeting expectations long enough to position for the second term?

The greatest uncertainty in the next several decades is that of war. War has long been the single greatest upheaval factor in history and also has provided governments with the single greatest rational to govern. "We will keep you safe" Obama's statement that he gets up every morning thinking about how to keep America safe and goes to bed every night thinking about how to keep America safe is a line straight from the Bush play book.

But it begs the issue: Can any President or military keep America safe?

Answer no.

Nuclear weapons have changed all that.
The dialogue below makes this point clear.

War and Peace

"There is in this world that eternal battle"
the General said 'between Good and Evil."

"There can be no compromise;
each nation needs living space
and those who follow Evil
will not hesitate
to take yours
and that means
some of the time
War."

"War is the ultimate expression
of Evil vs. Good
and inevitable."

Peace spoke:
"War is for those who profit from War
and every war ends in Peace
and diplomacy,
Why not skip the destruction and killing
save human lives
and go straight to the Peace?"

Nation-State spoke:
"Ah, you Peace, forget War
is more than the interval between
the Peace because War decides which people
will be free and which people will be oppressed.

Peace you misunderstand;
soldiers fight to preserve their country-men' lifestyles
their families
and those five dollar lattes."

"Ah, indeed in War and Peace
someone wins and someone loses." Nation-State said.

Peace spoke:
"Well, Nation-State, that used to be true
but not anymore.
Nuclear holocaust has no winners,
only losers."

"A radioactive planet
where no one can live
for a thousand years
is not victory
but massive defeat for everyone.

Nothing to celebrate."

"You"
Peace said
to the General
"cannot fulfill your main mission
which is to protect the population.
The foe you fight can blow up
all of their nuclear weapons
and the fall out will drift and kill
the rest of us
without even an attack."

"You soldiers have to learn new tricks.
You can't really protect us."

"All that is gone. You have to retire that side-gun
and sit at the diplomat's table."

"Peace" Peace said'
has come to depend upon successful social ecology
and restraining those who would have us kill ourselves
in order to preserve our lives."

Devolution Right and Devolution Wrong?

The answers, therefore, lie not so much with Obama, but with what I call the devolutionary forces already at work in American society and globally as well.

Devolution precepts are counter to the concentration of capital and power models we see where critical institutions become so interdependent and too big to fail threatening whole societies.

In massified societies with large populations, there is a natural tendency to evolve control to fewer and fewer individuals and to fewer and fewer institutions control of vital aspects of society. i.e. banks, governments, media, corporate entities.

Massification also brings power brokering, and raw political power acting directly upon the individual who becomes a powerless wage-earner.

The individual is swamped, subject to easy manipulation and is inundated with messages that her or she cannot really evaluate independently.

Small town face to face discussion and power-sharing modalities are rare. Most of us live in cities where we don't know who or congressional representative is or who is our Senator.

The reaction to concentration in the face of institutional collapses in the financial realm, in the political realm in many countries, sets us, I believe, on the path to devolution.

While many will try to patch up the large conglomerations in finance, government, social structures, churches etc. devolution will occur.

The only real question is whether that devolution will be disorderly, and virtually indistinguishable from collapse, or orderly and managed on an orderly basis.

Lets' take a few concrete examples. While the large banks are in trouble and can, as we see, collapse on a moments notice, the smaller regional and local banks do not, and have not.

We should plan for devolution back to local and regional banking. That system is more stable, better for consumers and the country as well.

Local bank "A" loans you money for your house and keeps your mortgage--not break it into twenty pieces and sell it to the Chinese, the Russians or whomever.

We will need large capital but that is another issue. Stability is the issue and local and regional financing and banking structures, we see, provide that.

Devolutionary governmental structures in tandem with building in more self-sustaining components seem more or less enviable. Here we have the Federal government handing out trillions of dollars to local and state governmental structures to do what those entities could have probably have done, if they had been allowed to keep the money, before sending it along to Washington,

This is not a states rights argument.

In a new devolution the financial goals are to use native funds and governmental funds to create new self-sustaining communities with green economies, which can give power back to the grid, create digital communities, eliminating the need for long communes, saving energy, time and dollars.

Is this possible?

Sure, we are not talking about every community but creating five or six technology enclaves. Apparently studies show that much of the wealth of developing and developed countries is generated by highly educated groups, living in mostly coastal or education intensive areas.

If these provide the economic drivers why not concentrate on these first with a focus on developing small and entrepreneurial supports. Small businesses provide most jobs in most economies.

The idea here is to focus on their development and accelerate the process and diffuse the results to the rest of the nation. But small is better, more manageable, and as we have seen, more sustainable.

But lets go to the summing up.

Whither America?

If not, a much darker scenario is clearly possible. If devolution is disorderly and accompanied by collapse what we are likely to see is described below in "The Muse-Whither America?"

The Muse- Whither America?

I asked the Muse Whither America?

"I see millions in the broken cities
crowding debt,
unhappiness.

I see family life un-affordable,
single parents struggling;

I see the children no longer able to afford the big houses
and the old ones abandon the homestead,
and crowd back to the cities.

The young ones can't find work;
it's five to a house.

The Americans, the British, the Italians
the Russians, all of Western Europe
can not
duplicate themselves and they perish
replaced by the poor ones from the East
and the South.

Economies will move toward barter exchange
because currency will fail,
replaced by new systems and gains in efficiency.

Government will devolve to less control
less bureaucracy;
more local control;
weak confederations instead.

All the world comes together to confront Destiny.
Whither the Planet?

But hope there is:
There will be in America
repatriation of the rural lands;
the abandonment of the cites
and massive building of rural technology-based enclaves;
smart technology driven, green based and self sufficient.

America's salvation there if they move quickly.

The village life returns.

Crafts replace portions of profit-based technology.

Old skills of self-sufficiency revive.

Nation states are weakened,
and cross national enclaves emerge
where ideas cross boundaries.

Real democracy will thrive in smaller settings.

This will be whether there is a precipitous sudden collapse or
planning for this.

Disaster will give us small enclaves
marauders and bandit bands
will leave the cities for the country-side
when the five day supply of food gives out;
creating enclaves fierce and violent.

Planning is the better way of course.
In your life-time son
40 years hence
this will be
but, which future.
will it be?

The Summing Up of the Summing Up:

The starkness of the assessment I have made above is gloomy but not without some hope. But first, this was historic election and I don't want to lose that thread. Historic for many reasons: it has forced American and western society in general to question some of it basic precepts:

Is continual economic growth a feasible model for our future? Perhaps not. The faith in continual progress and growth has been shaken. Hard to believe if you see major social and financial institutions failing and faltering and taking your life savings along with them in the fall.

Big capitalism doesn't look so rosy and no one seems to have an answer either on the reform side or on what would and can replace the system.

Hope and optimism for the future has stepped back a notch. Obama has put the world on notice that American consumer purchasing power can no longer fuel the world economies. So, what will? No one knows.

Faith in American institutions has been shaken. The anger is there looking for an outlet. That anger will have to be assuaged in the way Obama has—by increasing the debt to keep people in their homes, working and eating. if not social unrest will undo us.

Don't forget those thousands of Iraq soldiers coming home expecting a reward for defending America. The cost of their medical bills alone can break the American piggy bank.

So where are we? We are bidding our time, finger in the dyke until some solution set appears on the horizon. Cheered up enough? If not there's more.

We Need Social Reorganization and a New Paradigm Too:

In the United States we, I think, have to look to down-sizing our economy toward more self-sufficient communities, technology based, more efficient and more aimed toward the realities of a graying population, high energy costs and expensive labor--if you can get it—a small capitalism model to be created along side a much truncated large capitalism model—a mix.

Will this be the successful model of change? New Ideas Demand a New Vocabulary:

What ever the new solution-set for the future will be, it will be necessary to develop a new vocabulary to describe it. Describing the future in terms of past phrases and ideas has to be looked at carefully. So how do Eskimos explain to Americans their 150 different descriptions of snow when Americans only have 10 descriptions of snow?

Well it is not going to be easy.
Let's start with an outline. You cannot outline an entire future in this book. But here are the cliff-notes.

The belief in continual growth and larger and bigger everything is passé. The planet cannot sustain that kind of notion nor does it have the resources to sustain a high growth vector. Similarly, the corollary belief in continual progress has to likewise be re-conceptualized. We cannot afford continual progress because it costs too much. We have to forget the Cadillac and go for the Volkswagen. We also have to identify what is the driver is in this continually expanding growth model. Aside from greed, it is population-growth which in turn means jobs have to be found, food, labor for the engines of growth, troops for the increasingly difficult management job of managing a global system. Short version: no one is able to manage a global system. It simply runs amuck and has enormous weakness born of its very interdependence. The planet can't sustain the present population growth vector. Population we can control. But if we actually succeed in this area we threaten profits. Oh. So there will be political opposition and lifestyles will have to devolve. So here we come full circle.

Solution-Set:
We have to look to creating small, technologically smart smaller enclaves, towns with green sustainable technology, vegetable gardens; --targeted technology not trend--technology where every one has to have ever new toys is defunct, in my view.

Let's find something that works and stick with it. Don't upgrade, don't build for obsolesce. But what about jobs? No growth, no jobs for the young? True but only in the Western societies. The young will have to migrate to those emerging third world economies where the jobs will be-not to Europe, not the the United States.
Maybe learn Chinese.

As has been the case for centuries, individuals have to be ready to relocate to find work.

Decentralization also makes sense militarily; Ninety-percent of the US population living on 2% of the land, crowded into unworkable, unsustainable cities no longer makes any sense.

Back to the land with a technological, more sustainable base makes sense. Right now economically and militarily the American population is a sitting duck for a military attack and as it turns out an economic one as well.

Small, enclaves, means less travel, less energy use, less infrastructure costs and reunites the American family structure into a extended family model of close neighbors living close by.

Where to get the land? I'd suggest a new homestead act. There is plenty of land. But most is now owned or controlled by the US military, the interior department, or the utility companies.

Sure there is a battle there. But if the economy does fall or there is an extended depression, populations will do what they have always done: leave the cities and go back to land to survive. We will do that in this country in an orderly way or a disorderly way within the context of a sudden collapse. Let's plan for that transition, not be over-whelmed by it.

Concretely, start now to build pre-fab housing, Start now to put trailers in place new Orleans style. Start now to teach skills our grandfathers and grandmothers knew and we have lost. Most of us are so dependent we are helpless in case anything goes wrong in our over-technologized lives.

We cannot fix a TV. a car or larger housing appliances. Who even knows how these things work?

Rule: try to adopt a life-style where you can sustain what you depend upon. That is common sense.

It the end this model is one we have gone through in this country before. It is a mixed model where small enclaves of creativity are mixed with the larger capital model. The two can complement one another.

Small Towns May Have a Future But:

In America, Millennialism and the belief in the End Times continues to have hold in many small towns. The children sit in bedrooms contemplating what their futures will be. Parents, first in a generation see the American Dream slipping away and know that our leaders don't really have any answers that make sense, or even have been put forward.

I have made a few modest suggestions above, but new ideas are not easy to put forward. A new vocabulary is needed and the articulation of a new paradigm. But to get to that point new questions must be asked. And sadly at this point that has not occurred. Old questions around maintaining or restoring the current failed system are the ones being funded, put forth and being funded. And, they will have predictable results.

Small towns can be the nucleus of a restoration of sustainability. They perhaps can play a vital role. Micro-grants which are made to make developing country individuals can be looked at to see if they can be made to individuals' already in small towns or to individuals willing to relocate to small towns.

Small towns with new citizens have a chance for revival with direct subsidies. Direct subsidization has the advantage of being cheap, fast and the tourniquet is applied directly to the patient.

In any event, I believe giving up on small towns is not an option. They must be looked at in any revival scenario.

Politics and Leadership Anyone?

The rigors of leadership in interesting and crisis times, has been of course, a major topic in literature, especially with William Shakespeare who taught us that many great decisions in times of crisis hinge upon the personal traits of the decision-makers and his or her supporters.

The story below is one of a hero-leader, freshly elected and the struggles of leadership and the inter-personal relations which influenced his decision-making process in a time of crisis.

The personal and family side of Presidential decision-making often ignores these personal aspects, but note Hillary and Bill. Now we have Barack and Michelle. Note here that Michelle Obama can and will have an enormous influence on Obama.

This tale was written long before Obama arrived on the scene but it still has relevance in my estimation.

I have, in honor of the master, done it in a poor imitation of the Shakespearian style.

Politics

I. *Election*

His election was the on-rushing sun
impaling night
elevating him
propelling truths plain
beyond sight;
he was Hope to banish
and set aright
every ill;
to adjudicate each and every claim
their rushing joy
could ignite;
True Hope's awakened plebiscite
transforming the crowds' might
to Hard Justice reclaimed
whose sharp edges
would slice
to the core
of the body politic inflamed.
And bleed it's fever.

'I cannot' he said at the inaugural
'speak this proud heart,
I cannot utter or reveal
this ebullience born
whole cloth and sleek.

I cannot from these sputterings
steeped
in rhyme
adequately greet
perfection's own conjured touch
from which I reap
all this.

I am for you humility
rapturous this night
to be
riveted upon promises I'll keep
at each days end
where I will seek
each goal and nuance
foretold here;
til crime and its cousins Poverty,
Fear and Greed
shall shriek
and sulk away
far from here.

Tonight we dance with energy
loaned to us from Bright Intents
and vow to keep
our sights bent
upon honor's glorious ends.

We shall not forsake
nor misremember ends
here now we stake
and shall in time apprehend

the announced demise
of the evil three
Greed, Fear and Poverty.'
In thunder
the pact is born
amid a crowd swollen upon
new thoughts torn
from Hope's mouth.

Peter's words surely did excite
propelling himself and everyone
to height's horrid cloud
which adrift
was festooned with promised sweets
anointing the night resplendently-
Hope itself peaking-
plump with expectations
to exceed
wondrous mellifluous
Good Presents;

now a rising sun
then a setting phoenix
bejeweled now
but, later to be
crashed down
to Escheated
Miscommunications
and Properties.

So dizzy these heights
that the Fall will certain
see the deep depths

behind the curtains we draw
across intense intents
and proud decrees.

Sweet Elizabeth Peter's wife
cries softly foreseeing
Pride's Steel Locked Stance
being aware even then
that Democracy's Choice is iron
and will devour
the sublime
who mindlessly believe
now comes his time.

Rafael, the son
now proud to see
himself one day
in Father's place
thumps to the joy of it,
a time when justice gleaned
from Efforts Hope
rises from within him deep.

Monique, his intended
smiles-
herself ascended
to high regard-
sees in Rafael her love
a future bright

glowing shinier still
with new prospects;
power's appeal...

Her beauteous
quiet nature
belies an intelligence
yet beginning
but soon to gather
to critical mode
in one so tender
in her years.

The ministers all
with Peter now some years
see the dawning of New Time;
all pausing to celebrate
ignoring
all trouble and obscured
nearby chimeras.

But joy drunkens
swollen eyes befog
the on-rushing times
and addicted
we all succumb
to revelry
and numb,
notice not
moorings loosed,
which in time
set adrift our oared skiff
rendering certainty moot.

Precious Love unsure,
and Pain now paused
will likely be ladled to each

and every one
acute.

II.
Loving Too

That Night She:
'Your sugar eyes
move my soul
You have me in my secret place
my rivers run full for you;
in enveloping heat
lifting me with your soft kiss
I take you inside
to fit
swollen against
my oval space;
I admit
that this is the deep secret me.
I open to all of you
my sweet,
settling love upon
my pillow keep
where whispered calls
beckon my pleasure-sleep.

Our hearts bind now
promises and ecstasies."

He:
'I am swept away to aching degree
for you
my thickness tingles
and seats itself
gingerly.

Without you
I am rudderless.
Without you
I have nothing achieved.
Without you,
my way streaks
forward
tremblingly
bereft,
absent love's crucial pleat
in my heart's linings,
which with you
I'm rendered complete.

Touch us now Simplicity
man to woman
lover to lover's
fulsome esprit.
So gripped we,
softly gasping,
moving together till short day-light
chartered one to the other
joined this to that
perfect destiny welded tight
two together at the sensual site
spinning beyond midnight's
Magic Transfixion.

'I love you' she cried. 'in all ways'
'I love you' he said
in double receipt.
The two wrapped round together
each bonded symbiotically

one to give more to the other
each to give more than given
both to grow larger than
each one's talents alone could abide
each to exceed beyond
a solo effort striven.

Love's Test moves
to achieve
and go
far from the mundane goal
beyond even Hope's
stated given.

Circumstances now all in place
Opportunity secure in state
quivering Excitement's Face
glows.
Now begins this human race.

Two lovers there initiate
the Crown of State in Sexual Space
these things preceded by you see
lovely love and nights embrace.
So much in human history
is bedroom born;
so much human history therefore:
War and Peace.

III. *War Reckoning*

Peter's hand in the years was bent toward peace
and he
in inclination's way
sought to avoid conflict
so much so that he did not see
in the fifth year John's dark rise from the East
till that day arrived in which he
had to decide
upon War or Peace.

Elizabeth's eyes could see that Destructions Fear
was nigh and upon them.
She counseled:
'He has taken lands which did not belong with him
he flanks you on the left
even now at the river's end.
You must quell this trend.
His armies advance and descend
till late to the sword
you'll have to jockey
your men
at the very kitchen door!

The maps' edge creeps
close to our very walls.
Your minister's quake-
nay sleep-
yet you do not hear, see
or speak."

Alliances like marriages can quickly wear
if the habit develops where one loves war
and the other craves peace.

"Grasp the jaw bone of the ass" she said
"and strike now.
Later then
enjoy the peace.
Otherwise I fear
there will be no calm
except that of the bloody hand,
a muted shriek
and lost, sad, opportunity.
Hope herself will weep.
Now, now' she said
'is the time to employ resources
amass your leadership;
you could expend a small pittance's gold
and a colossal treasure reap!
You my love have too much regard
for harmony.
Efforts' just return is what you seek."

But Peter was not persuaded thus
his way was gentler still
Foreboding's Shroud gathered round his brow
quietly shrill.

"I could raise the taxes and
recruit the army and move my chessmen
'cross topography
only to find unrest and booty

be taken from me
by those left behind to guard the nest.

Nay I worry most
of the Enemy Within.
Hollow victories
and homeland defeats
are equally cheap.
I would have in this, fired the first shot
only to feel the pain in my own feet!

Why, my God, is it that the advisor is always bold
when the advisor is not the one to pay
in consequences and gold?

I am leadership
whose charge is to think
before I become bloodied
upon the jaws of victory
then only by hindsight
to see the irony
of sudden, unanticipated retreat.

No I will council with my own destiny
and look to see how to act in circumstance.
All that is clear is uncertainty
where potentially what lurks for me
is homeland treachery
and deceit
concocted behind my own lines
from fickle friends who'll turn on me.
Then all I'd bring home
is that which is not victory

but a hollow stampede
bereft of the prize I seek;
no triumphant victory.

I sit now to think.
Risk is the horse we ride
and saddleless
I don this night
Caution's Cloak
and my own bromides.

Elizabeth's eye was steeled blue
Impatience's Glint
within.
Peter's hesitation for her
took the bold
and denuded it
behind fearful thought
and adverse risk;
he thought not to act
but to think;
not strike
but to stare at opportunity blatant
and blink.

Rather than speak her mind
she choose to eschew
biting conflict
uttering only
"Yes dear. All you say is true."

IV. *Counsel of War*

Peter yet with his own counsel of war
resolved to manage his risk
and send his son Rafael
to collect the army's taxation list.
Peter least his homeland fears come true
surmised that
he Peter
would be close
to the rear
to forestall his homeland enemies caveat
and at once to foil the Trojan Horse
which could crush victory won
on distant soil.
The day Rafael had his list
and gathered himself to leave
Elizabeth hovered by
in grief
imploded with the belief
that Peter at once
had opted to sacrifice
her son
to whom she had over the years
grown to cleave
more closely it seemed
than to Peter even,

whose preoccupations
had caused her silent strife
and inward grown.

She had plunged all love and grief
into the young son
who now, instead, prepared to leave.

"Promise me you'll not risk injury
rather, gather the guards round your group
and protect this countries future state.
Honor this
by oath agree
and this night I'll rest serene."

Rafael:
"I am not given Mother to lead
by retreat
my place is at the head
and to indeed exceed
at the forefront lines that meet
in the face of our enemies."

She:
"You do not have to do this
you can return to me
and take your place where the need
will be greatest here in our own country.
Say to your father and I will support
there is no need to risk your young life
wastefully, needlessly."

Peter heard this from his approach
and incensed he roared:
"You will not object to decisions of state.

You will not seek to undo or abate
that which is decided by me.

This boy's time is now to leave
neither to cleave to your wiles
nor from my own will.

Away from both of us lies his formation
and destiny
That my dear is the reason he was born to us-
to leave.
Neither one of us can sacrifice him to our need,
to clutch him too close to
you nor me.
He goes,
that is best
eschewing even my own desires
and even your anxieties."

She:
"No, you do not use cold reason here.
No, you do not rationalize this sacrifice
to an empty state craft device.
This is not mechanical
but yours and my son's life!
Do not send him deathward there
Do not press life from him
with marching bands
and horns and hymns."

Rafael:
"I will not be treated like this!

Mother you want guarantees and security
where none is possible for me.
You, Father
all you see is glory and duty
yet it is love which drives our solders
not booty.
I am a symbol and indeed
love is not mine to receive
but if I die
it will be because I am committed
and trapped
by the circumstance
we weave
in pursuing our goals and needs
that this line of soldiers marching means.

Yes, we shall grieve death's lot
perhaps mine
and then it will be over
and we shall lift a cup
and move on
no lingering memory sups.

I will go as you request Father
because I have chosen duty
But I am not the reasons I leave
I am the person leaving.
I am not reason's ploy
I am Rafael
I'll fight for friends and you

for our family
and those who understand a young mans need
to achieve that which is unutterable
to matter in the scheme of things.
I meander;
but my course is to straightaway
to leave.

Father:
"Whatever is in you
I understand leave you must-
time flees."
Monique to whom Rafael
was to marry
caught him
at the door
and aside spoke
quietly.
She:
"I am unable to persuade you
nor can I beseech any caring feeling
strong enough to avert this.
 I am filled with a desperate foreboding.
Go, but, only later my sweet.
Surely there can be no harm
in delaying a week
death itself to cheat."
He:
"I cannot shrink away from this
as others themselves gather arms.
Lead I must and you should understand
some things a woman must do alone
and similarly therewith a man.

You do not understand,
your heart always reaches.
In life and even love
in some things we are alone
even amid our comforts
cocoons and hearthstones."

Outside:
Horns Blow
He:
"I must go."
She:
"How silly it is
to me to see
that so many are willing to die
for baubles ribbons and trinkets."
He:
"Understand,
if I must die
I shall do so with your name on my breath,
and within me
though my heart be wounded
you shall know
you are my most felt one
and wounded there
know that even at death's door
my love for thee in genuine
shall not be stayed
and will remain strong."

She:
I shall pleasure receive
hope for your safe return
and yet
even if it must be so
reach you
beyond even death's door.
Here on these lips
plant this kiss
for relief from even
cold death's grip
and return you safe revived,
home to me.'
With this they embraced
staunch memory
etched on mouth
and face
and Rafael
moved out
in formation haste.

So, there were the colors
and departures
long lines and battleships
weeping eyes,
and goodbyes
long looks and promises;
and off thousands sailed
each without travail
till iron glory upon them all prevailed
in battle greens and blues
in clamorous scenes

of smoke and hue
of faces blank and wet
from battle cries
and wounds rosette
from shock and battle deaths
this swept down suddenly
on many and the few
who spun from blows spent
to pirouette
falling listlessly
to ground and history
whose names read once
in letters due
to family, lovers, children
and those who would not forget.
Some returned;
this one wrapped in glory
and another in despair's
costume.
So it was with Rafael,
a battle line snaps
and he
lost a limp
in the Slashing Grim
hacked away
while in the saddle
yet, and he persisted bleeding throughout
till coma-like he fell
grounded
sidelined within
sight of victory
a lump upon the pocked ground

he lay awaiting
rescue sounds
his pain exceeding
till his mind passed away
to dead faint
eyes rolled up
to heaven,
silence now decrees,
one's body lumped
upon the battlefield to bleed.
"Monique," is the silent cry
on his lips parting
"all for you even this
is not enough.
My love grows
even as I die departing
this earthly ground,
my love for you
now more than then
stronger
and more profound."
His first words on revival
were "did we prevail"?
The answer back,
"no sire
defeat nor victory was ours-
stalemate."

V.
War

That day split the times:
Booty not
nor glory.
War's initiation
stripped the grace
from Innocent's eyes
and often heard thereafter
the cry
to what therefore and why?
"To protect our land
peoples and crew
our children, women
and all those whom we love."
So home them all
with stories true and tall
to sit
recuperating
till another time
when the battle
might resume
and again the clarion call.
Ghost battles for some will loom
belching new flame young men and boys,
girls and youth
new flesh to consume.
Yet repeated this so many times
the need cannot be doubted
sometimes it is our fate

to fight, and die
thereby doubt itself to be routed;
stand, be true its said
and be counted.
We in the end must support
those who took to hand
stout arms and went
far far away
to fight against
our foes and enemies
despite all consequence.

All energies spent
Rafael's limb lay bent
slashed and soiled
by sword's tip
was gathered up
and delivered home to Monique who
could not at first contemplate
the view
of him a returned
broken patriot.
For days she sat disconsolate,
her rooms a duty gray
rearranging the folds of her
simple dress
carefully.
The thin arms moved
only to grasp
tea served occasionally
by Marion
the one who visited with news
and solace in compendium

from those who loved her
together as one.
Finally Monique was able
to reluctantly agree to see Rafael
still unclear how glory could be
lived on the veranda, in the house
or in the street
wheelchair bound.
His wheelchair rolled into their rooms
a year late from war and feats
and indecision
from Monique.
The two
as with the war
in these first moments
were together
in neither victory nor defeat
but then only began
an interlude
now life wound down to the concrete
and mundane need;
a young man neither totally incapacitated
nor dead
yet alive,
yet still
brimming with desires,
wishes hopes and dreams
all now in caveats
metaphors,
and apostrophes.

Rafael now sat then
mirror reflected
ignoring Monique
who languished hesitantly
while he
inspected limp limbs
realizing for the first time
while she was there
in malingering toward the first night
he did not know how he would do
what he couldn't do
for his wife to be,
how love could translate
how arms could encapsulate
how his genitalia could move
could perform feats
other men do.

His younger that his years face
glowed white
as she approached from across the room.
Yet 23 and hands small
she placed them close
by the collar
of his jacket
still worn from the War's end
and spoke:
"I am so so sorry that I have not
been able to be with you
it was shame that held me back.
No it's not shame for you but for me.
After the first week I was ashamed that

I had not been to see you
and the longer it grew
the more difficult it was for me
to move
toward the decision that
I'd missed.
And the shame grew
till paralyzed
I could not move
from my rooms
till the time grew
beyond
endurance yet I sat
in my rooms
loving you
but, paralyzed."

"I am so sorry that my humanness
surely hurt and harmed you
I know you have for yourself
your own endurances.
I only ask
you forgive me now
and let pass
what was for me
inexcusable
grief driven
leaving me
unable to offer a true excuse,
uttering now only words oblique,
to hide myself behind
opaque at the door."

Rafael:
"Oh Monique I have these many weeks
given every thought to you
and more
my soul leaped at any image
reminiscent.
So when the plunge took my leg
and homeward bound
I feel a small relief
that again this tattered heart
would view
that face which sustained me
through
hell fire and death dealt
crushing blows.
Oh I saw men fall
shattered it seemed by inward
bombs
eyes now opened wide
still seeing
yet already gone-
beyond feeling.
And painful cries-
heroics to be sure-
all there in amid the many and the few.
Never tell, I think, the details there
for they do indeed, far exceed
explanation and belief
if you were not on the field
to see how
so much ingenuity
in war and arms

goes with the sole intent
of mayhem and bodily harm
to young ones who are often sent
armed only with fresh-minted
inexperience.
And then they fall
torn from them
the veil that sheltered
their innocence.
All we believe Monique
screams
this is the essence of injustice
yet all of history's testament
is each era
must
confront and commit
the scene again over and over."

 V11.
That first night he lay in repose
the first night she gave him
all;
the first night suspended them
between the lagging conversation
after love's glow
into questioning
about what to do
at 23; she unsure of life's
meanderings
He wondering
"How can I be a man with thee
you have most to do
to bring to me to the point to sate

overcoming meager desire's weaken state
How can love compensate?"
She:
"It can
my love
give me time to suggest
how devotion's arrow is stronger
still than body limbs.
You are the man I love
and now surely there is this test
for us now
but all years ahead
will allow
my will
to love whole
as we are
to manifest.
Surely now we are challenged to make of it our best.
And best it shall be
because together we are whole
and all we need to be.
To begin
and beginning is what we are about
no doubt
we have all we need
to go forth
and succeed
at whatever passes us.
Do not for one flicker doubt
I shall be here
to carry out what ever the load be."

And so Rafael and Monique
made their peace
for the time being.

VIIII.

Elizabeth Grieves

Elizabeth took to bed
and did not grieve initially
rather she lay in state it seems
rigid in her mien
and unwilling to take a single step
fueled so to speak by small amusements
and stimulants.
To Peter she would state
"I warned of this outcome and portent
yet unheeded you allowed all to go forth
and now all for me is grief bedridden where I will die"
she said "a thousand grieving deaths."
"You cannot' Peter said "lay here
each day arms raised
piling lament upon lament"

 "I am dead to you now"

"Is this my punishment"

"I am wife no more"

"You must do more"

"I am total done"

"Life cannot pass us by-you must rise"

"If I could only cry"

"You are my wife"

"Wife no more-I'm lost"

Do you want Angelica?"

"Utter not that name to me
you know that is something I forbid
She left us now many years and now
you would bring her up to me."?

"I am desperate placed to offer whatever
I can to move you from this state.
Tell me what I must do. I am alone here-
out there without you."
She:
"Peter acclimates.
I am down here for the long time.
Rise I would if I could
but all this was a fatal brush
with more than I can handle.
Perhaps it was the war's end,
or Rafael whose very life lies in ashes.
There is only so much
my mind can take
There is a line beyond which we all break
I fear my boundaries have been ripped,
sanity reels and slips away
from me sometimes
more often it seems more frequently
and frighteningly I grasp
at darken maps

looking for a tiny blip
to let me know I still exist
underneath there in the catastrophe.
Hollow voices call, my own I think
Rafael, help me, help me.'
Peter felt he was slipping
from his own grip
and could not in these early days
bring himself to carry on
without the strength
Elizabeth brought.
His drug ways increased
his heart would cease
in odd moments
wherein he would have to remind himself
to breathe.
But tragedy was not done yet
because more befell this bedraggled set.
It concerns footsteps light
which Elizabeth lay down one fateful night
leaving her bed
renting her vow
and traipsed her way by corridor
to enter unannounced
Rafael's door.
Monique drew her eyes from sleep
and peered into the darken room
awaken by swishing sounds
of rushing cloth and flowing gown

to dimly see Elizabeth kissing Rafael
who still maintained his deepest sleep.

The hands drew a tender place across
his still sleeping face
a kiss
falls only to retrace
followed on by a full embrace.
Monique called to Elizabeth
her voice barely a whisper
but paralyzed she could not move
or be heard by Elizabeth who
had given Rafael all her nocturnal attention.
Now he roused himself from sleep
and face on with her that sought to reap
more kisses planted upon his countenance
His hand rose
still sleepy amid
the attentions being paid him.
Now it was then that a muffed yelp escaped
from Monique who again stifled yet another yell
when Elizabeth heard and noticed her.
Coming from Rafael she slowly made
to Monique a tosseled slow approach.
Her face was dimmed in bedroom light
and Monique could only see the partial smile
whereon she said 'Hello my dear, how I envy
you. I so desperately appreciate how you have
sought to heal this Rafael.
She knelt to kiss Monique upon the lips
and stole softly away
leaving in her wake
a shaken two
Rafael and Monique.

Both staring in the dim light and wondering
'What and wherefore
was this'

IX.
Angelina

But then
amid this time
Angelina came through
contacted by Peter
hoping Elizabeth would rip aside
that tissue placed
between her grim despair
which had effaced
the joy Peter now missed
so much.
Many years in exile deep
Angelina sometimes could keep
at bay insanity.
Slow motion she
mounted the coach.

The ride was a silent one
Angelina reluctant to speak
or emote
and unsure after these many years
how her words would be taken in,
what affect her own feelings
would project
afraid of her own chagrin

that her father had greeted her
so listlessly
after so many years.

And so resentment then
and anger later
and the returning cycle
begins
again.

What mix here of politics
of family, love, death and fear
propels Ships of State
and the familial?

Are we not Captains of the Guard
but also Billy Boy or Fathers Son?
Is sweet Monique the small girl first
before she drank the Princess Milk
to slack the thirst which is learned?
only second
not first.
So entwined these destines mixing
all in human frailties
and Human Destiny
such fragile vessels
swing our Fates'
 Door knobs and Hinges.

　　　END

www.ingramcontent.com/pod-product-compliance
Lightning Source LLC
Chambersburg PA
CBHW060615290526
45793CB00001B/32